THROUGH
STUDENTS'
EYES

THROUGH STUDENTS' EYES

Combating Racism in United States Schools

Karen B. McLean Donaldson

Foreword by Sonia Nieto

Westport, Connecticut
London

Library of Congress Cataloging-in-Publication Data

Donaldson, Karen B. McLean.
  Through students' eyes : combating racism in United States schools
/ Karen B. McLean Donaldson ; foreword by Sonia Nieto.
    p.   cm.
  Includes bibliographical references and index.
  ISBN 0–275–95478–1 (alk. paper). —ISBN 0–275–95818–3 (pbk.)
  1. Discrimination in education—United States.   2. Racism—United
States.   3. Multicultural education—United States.   4. Arts—Study
and teaching (Secondary)—United States.   I. Title.
  LC212.2.S65   1996
  370.19'342—dc20   96–10432

British Library Cataloguing in Publication Data is available.

Library of Congress Catalog Card Number: 96–10432
ISBN: 0–275–95478–1
       0–275–95818–3 (pbk.)

First published in 1996

Praeger Publishers, 88 Post Road West, Westport, CT 06881
An imprint of Greenwood Publishing Group, Inc.

Printed in the United States of America

The paper used in this book complies with the
Permanent Paper Standard issued by the National
Information Standards Organization (Z39.48–1984).

10 9 8 7 6 5 4 3 2 1

This book is in memory of Randy Cortez who was killed in a car accident July 1996 at the age of 21. Randy was a key participant in the study that made this book possible. He was an excellent student and honorable young man who was committed to reducing racism in schools and society. He coined our study group SARIS (Students against Racism in Schools) and looked forward to this publication spreading the views of young people as well as SARIS chapters being started by students throughout the United States. Thank you Randy for all of those you touched and convinced that racism hurts us all. Your presence will be missed but your spirit and strength will live on in those of us who brave to stand against racial injustice.

Karen Donaldson
September 9, 1996

Contents

Foreword

Multicultural education has developed as a discipline in important ways since its modern-day reappearance in the early 1970s. This growth has been especially impressive in the 1990s, and it will doubtless continue given the convergence of a number of conditions in our society: the dramatically increasing pluralism in schools and communities; a recent commitment on the part of a growing number of teacher education programs to include a more focused approach to diversity; and the burgeoning number of scholars devoting their professional lives to research in multicultural education, especially those from Latino, African American, Asian American, and Native American backgrounds who were almost nonexistent just two decades ago. These conditions bode well for the discipline. Although multicultural education was perceived as a fad or passing fancy just a few years ago, it is now building a solid base in theory and research.

In spite of the tremendous growth in the conceptual development of multicultural education, however, there continues to be a dearth of research that focuses on practices and approaches for making schools and classrooms truly multicultural. The research reported by Karen Donaldson in this book is among a small but growing and vital number of studies that will help fill this void. It will help answer questions such as: What does antiracism mean in practice? How does multicultural education fit into the entire school curriculum? What can teachers do to engage students in discussions of pluralism and prejudice?

By addressing these concerns, this book provides a meaningful service to classroom teachers, administrators, and scholars interested in expanding their understanding of multicultural education and its role in curriculum reform in general.

But Karen Donaldson's book does much more than this. One of the greatest criticisms lodged against multicultural education in the past has been its tendency, if not in theory at least in practice, to trivialize differences and thus generate a kind of "feel-good" pedagogy by including only superficial ethnic tidbits and decontextualized "contributions of others" to the curriculum. It is not surprising that this should happen given the very limited examples of in-depth and serious attention in the curriculum to structural barriers to equality in our schools and society. It is far easier to concentrate on ethnic celebrations or "Brown heroes" taken out of historical context. *Through Students' Eyes* confronts in a direct way such trivialization by presenting in detail a significant example of an arts-based, student-centered approach to including racism in the curriculum. The focus on racism is especially timely when we consider the growing violence in and out of schools, the disappointing results of school reform efforts of the past decade, and the unfulfilled promise of equal educational opportunity for many of our youth. Young people confront violence every day, and by neglecting to discuss racism, teachers lose a golden opportunity to engage students in conversations that consider one of the primary factors that lead to it.

Young people are demanding to discuss and learn about issues that are important in their lives, and racism is often at the top of the list. As is clear from Karen Donaldson's study, prejudice and discrimination are pivotal issues in the lives of many students at all levels of schooling. Yet the curriculum to which they are exposed daily seldom touches on these concerns. How racism can become material for the curriculum is presented in detail in this book. Nevertheless, this is not a step-by-step recipe for including racism in student learning, but instead an example of a particular curriculum that was developed by teachers and students themselves in their own context. This, too, is a considerable lesson for teachers, for it reinforces once again the crucial truth that curriculum needs to begin where students are at in order to build on their learning.

Lessons can be learned from the teachers in this study as well, and these lessons can be used to reform teacher education in colleges and universities as well as in professional development efforts at the school level. The fact that a substantial number of the teachers in the study denied or downplayed the role that racism plays in the lives of their students (and that many of them changed their views as a result of the actual curriculum development in which they took part) is a key lesson for those of us involved on a daily basis with preparing the nation's teachers. Issues such as racism and other forms of both personal and institutional discrimination can no longer be ignored in our courses and workshops, but need to become central concerns in addressing the problem of educational failure. For both students and teachers, having the space to discuss these issues is a lesson in democracy itself because democratic principles based on platitudes are no substitute for honest and open discussions that can lead to difficult, but in the long run, more honest depictions of how democracy works in action.

Karen Donaldson reminds us that young people are deeply concerned about fairness and equality. This book stands as an eloquent proclamation of the deep understanding they have about the impact of racism on their lives, the value of education for their future, and the important role they can have in creating more inclusive schools. It is one of the few books that celebrate the words, the visions, and the dreams of youth. Perhaps through the example it provides, all of us—teachers, parents, and students—can encourage all young people to become critical thinkers and to be energized and empowered by their schooling. What more could we want for our students?

Sonia Nieto
University of Massachusetts
Amherst, Massachusetts
January 1996

A Personal Note

Who am I, and why have I dedicated more than twenty years of teaching and research to working with students to combat racism in schools? I am an African American woman, mother, wife, artist, and educator, and I have been affected by the symptoms of racism. Throughout my life I have experienced second-class treatment of my ethnic group. As a student, I was traumatized by racist attitudes that resulted in an inadequate education and low self-esteem. Although I am now a professor of education with a doctoral degree, the road to this achievement was long and painful.

When I was ten my dad died of cancer. After his death, our family was forced to move from our African American middle-class community to cheaper housing, the "Projects." My mother could no longer afford our Catholic school education; she therefore enrolled us in a program that bused inner-city youth to schools in the suburbs. I was the first of my siblings to go. Each morning I would leave home at 5:30. It would still be dark outside and I would often have to fight off the rats with rocks by our dumpsite to get to my stop. My two-hour ride would consist of passing dilapidated buildings and liquor stores in my community, to seeing luxurious homes with swimming pools and great landscaping. At school, students and teachers would pat my afro (hair) and ask me to sing and dance black songs. They would always ask me to repeat my black vernacular because it tickled them to hear it. Although this school was state of the art, I disliked going there. I wondered why we couldn't have good schools in our own community. I begged my mother to return me to my own community school, and she did. My neighborhood high school was close to being condemned; the first-floor staircase had collapsed into the basement level and was never repaired. Nevertheless, I was delighted to go there and be among the friends I had grown up with. During the three years that followed, I found most of my teachers uncaring toward students of color. Most of the time they found "busy work" for us to do; one teacher had us handwrite each chapter from our textbook. This was the only lesson we did in his class for the entire school year. Ultimately, I had to work and pay tutors to help me through my beginning college years. It was difficult and I resented not receiving a good foundational education.

Twenty-five years later, my own children are experiencing racism in schools. For example, as a fourth-grader, my eldest daughter ran home in tears because she was called a "nigger" by a white student. It is important to share these experiences at the outset, because they are the experiences of many people of color attending schools during and after the passage of Title VI of the Civil Rights Act of 1964 (P.L.88-352), a piece of legislation that many assumed would end racism in schools. Those of my generation bear witness that racism exists in schools, and that it is a form of abuse from which many victims never fully recover. To avoid the continued abuse of students, we must acknowledge the presence of racism in schools and work diligently to make a change.

In this personal note I have revealed my passion for wanting to help eradicate racism in schools, but I have gone beyond passion to action. This book is filled with research and antiracist projects; much of it is through students' eyes because they are the recipients of racist treatment and can best share how such treatment affects student learning and development. Too often victims of racism are blamed for being overly sensitive, and are therefore often ignored. In response to this dilemma, I emphasize my formal research in the book, as opposed to my passion, so that readers can acquire the information necessary to understand the harm and pervasiveness of racism in our schools and ways to combat it.

Acknowledgments

This book is dedicated first and foremost to the many youth who made it possible. Their commitment and self-determination was an inspiration for me to carry out my writing and research. Young people are amazing. They have many social concerns that often go unrecognized. I am grateful that I was given the opportunity to learn and document their views.

I immensely appreciate the following colleagues who consented to review this book: Sonia Nieto, Theresa McCormick, Beverly Tatum, Carl A. Grant, and Carlie Tartakov. Sonia Nieto, who graciously agreed to do the foreword, guided and encouraged me throughout my effort to produce a book that highlights the sentiments of students regarding racism in schools. Sonia Nieto, Theresa McCormick, and Carlie Tartakov reviewed the book in its beginning stages and gave incredible feedback; without their assistance I may have given up on such an arduous task. I am also grateful to my editor, Lynn Taylor, for her patience, and to my friend and unofficial editor, Anita Rollins.

I must especially thank those who made the Teacher Project research possible. This preliminary research gives added hope to the goal of reducing racism in schools. I also thank the numerous teachers who gave their time during the study. Teachers such as Wayne Clinton, Dr. Dwight Herold, Barbara Jefferson (principal), and Dr. Suzanne Mendelson (associate principal), who have demonstrated their undaunting commitment to eliminating racism in schools, have made the Teacher Project worthwhile. In addition, I am very grateful to my graduate research assistants (provided by the Iowa State University Graduate Minority Student Affairs Office) Anthony Stevens (study analyst), Maurizio Visani, and James McShay for their hard work in preparing and disseminating the study instruments: and to my department chair, Ann Thompson, who granted me research release time. I thank the Research Institute on Studies in Education (RISE)/Iowa State University for assisting me in this process also. I further extend my appreciation to Mary Worthy, and the Diversity Consultant Network members for being investigators and antiracist education specialists for the project.

I cannot end my acknowledgments without mentioning my family. I thank my husband, Christopher Donaldson, and children, Wayne, Nyanda, Devin, Chris Jr., Courtney, and my mentee daughter, Lavonne Carson, for their love and encouragement, and last but not least my mom, Marie McLean, who has been an avid reader and supporter of my work.

THROUGH
STUDENTS'
EYES

Introduction

Racism in U.S. Schools: Crutch, Myth, or Reality?

> Racism, ever since I was a child, has had a negative effect
> on me. It's always made me feel depressed and had a
> negative effect on my grades. I always did bad in my
> classes where I had teachers that were racist or that were
> always putting me down because of my color; well, that's
> the same thing.
>
> Interview: tenth-grader, Donaldson, 1993

For those who have seldom been victims, it is difficult to imagine the
pain and suffering caused by discrimination due to race. Those who
lack understanding of racism often accuse the victims of being overly
sensitive "whiners" who look for special treatment because they are
too lazy to achieve on their own initiative.

If racism only exists in the minds of the lazy, why do students
who are high achievers have painful stories of racism to share? For
example, sixteen-year-old Charissa, who was named a 1995 *Newsweek*
scholar (*Daily Tribune*, March 3, 1995), stood before her classmates
and delivered her paper, "The Difficulties Minority Students
Encounter in Predominantly White Schools." Many of the males in
the class criticized Charissa for writing such a paper. They made
statements such as, "You're just another crying black person looking
for a crutch." Charissa, who had come to me at the university for ad-
vice on how to get her paper to appeal to the white males in her class,

attempted to address their accusation logically: "I am an honors student. Why would I need a crutch?" She went on to say, "I am just trying to share with you how racism hurts; a perfect example is right now." With her self-esteem shaken, feeling distraught by her peers' ignorance, Charissa anxiously counts the days until she will be out of school permanently (Interview, Donaldson, May 1995). Following this and many other incidents of racism, Charissa chose not to graduate with her high school class and applied for early college entrance. Three months later, she is still trying to get over the racism she experienced. She commented that "The racism in my high school really lowered my self-esteem. It has taken a lot of prayer and support from my mom and friends to rebuild my self-confidence" (Interview, Donaldson, August 1995). Is racism in schools a crutch, myth, or reality?

This book was written for practicing schoolteachers, school administrators, other educators, researchers, preservice teachers, high school students, parents, and the general public to challenge the assumption that racism has been eradicated within our nation's schools, or that it has minimal or no effect on student learning. It was also written to challenge those who believe that racism is used as a crutch to enable students to make excuses for failure. Through exploring the experiences with racism of high academic achieving students, I address these misconceptions.

Many U.S. school personnel do not view racism as a major deterrent to the learning of minority students. In fact, educators often assume that racism is only moderately present or does not exist at all in the school setting. Yet, on the contrary, throughout the country an analysis of numerous school systems in the recent past discloses racist and violent acts targeted toward students of color. For example, Stover (1990) cites two recent incidents: in California, secondary students displayed a white doll dressed in a Ku Klux Klan robe and a black doll with a noose around its neck; in Mississippi, secondary students displayed Confederate flags during a black history program. In Massachusetts, a secondary teacher wrote a widely publicized racist letter about her students (Branchard [pseudonym] Public Schools, 1992, pp. 32–39), and a student Ku Klux Klan member recruited fellow students, held rallies, and harassed the only black high school teacher in the district, who after twenty-five years of service resigned because she feared for her life (Transcript Newspaper, 1992). In

Alabama, deep racial divisions came out when the principal of a high school threatened to cancel the prom to prevent interracial dating and told a biracial student that her birth was a mistake (Gross & Smothers, 1994). These are just a few examples of racist acts occurring in schools in recent times.

Repeatedly, racism manifests itself in classrooms through the ignorance of individual teachers and administrators as well as through institutionalized racism. Students of color, in both urban and suburban schools, are subjected to inequality through the smaller amount of instructional time given, biased texts and curricula, harsh sanctions (suspension and detention), lowered teacher expectations, and teacher/administrator and school denial of racist actions (Murray & Clark, 1990; Pine & Hilliard, 1990).

Racism also manifests itself as an internal struggle in many students. Students of color may choose not to be seen as high achievers because to do so they would be considered "sellouts" or "white-wanna-bes" (Donaldson, 1994; Fordham & Ogbu, 1986). The same rule applies in many predominantly white suburban schools, where students of color struggle not to conform to the limiting Eurocentric education and attitudes to which they are exposed. This refusal to buy into mainstream cultural values, and educators' refusal to reward diverse cultural values, often contribute to school failure. In addition, some students resort to camouflaging their efforts to achieve, and thus lead a double life. These identity conflicts can be overwhelming and cause emotional damage to many youth.

The violence and hatred that undergird racism, which took root in the European colonization of the Americas for the purpose of power and profit, support the interethnic hostility that is found among many cultural groups. Racism has become an infectious disease from which no group is immune; the victim, who is most often a person of color, is reactive and resentful of white oppression. Frequently, these victims take out their resentment on members of their own racial group because of the inaccessibility of the real culprits, those who are in power. Although many ethnic groups have been antagonistic toward one another for centuries, the "new racism" of the United States, in most cases, is the greater influence.[1] Cultural hostility, where the victim in the society becomes the victimizer at school or in the local neighborhood, has become blatant at the institutional level. School systems report frequent interethnic fights, such as in the case of a Los Angeles school where five fights were reported during a two-month period between Japanese-American and Korean-American students (Stover, 1990). Teachers have cited incidents of interethnic victimization (i.e., black-on-black prejudice) between Haitian-born and American-born black students in the Miami school system, and of Latin-on-Latin prejudice between Puerto Rican and Dominican students in the New York system (Stover, 1990).

The focus of learning in school is deterred repeatedly by racism (Murray & Clark, 1990; Pine & Hilliard, 1990). Although racism in its many forms affects the learning abilities of all students, it is an especially significant barrier to students of color. If students of color do not feel safe, academically challenged, or included in the curriculum, they will not produce at their most efficient or creative capacity. With the burden of racism, many students of color tune out, burn out, act out, or drop out of school. Institutionalized racism helps breed high school dropouts because it damages the self-esteem of students, as well as influences their educational motivation and feelings of belonging. Studies show that dropout rates are substantially higher in urban areas, in public schools, and among minority youth (LeCompte & Dworkin, 1991). These higher dropout rates can be attributed in part to racism in schools (Clark, 1993; Fine, 1991). A growing body of evidence reveals that the perceptions of children regarding whether the school environment is fair and supportive is often the key to whether the children succeed in school (Murray & Clark, 1990).

The implications of racism in society as a whole are tremendous. Each year it is estimated that $260 billion will be lost in earnings and foregone taxes because of youth who will be unemployable (LeCompte & Dworkin, 1991). U.S. wages will decrease as the need for social services, such as welfare and the criminal justice system, critically increase and affect the nation's economy (LeCompte & Dworkin, 1991). Violence and tension will grow at even higher rates and cripple many more communities. Without a new generation of productive workers, the United States will no longer be able to maintain its position with regard to global economics.

Education plays an important role in the future of the United States. The goal for primary and secondary education is as follows: "Every school in America will ensure that all students learn to use their minds in order to prepare them for responsible citizenship, further learning, and productive employment in a modern society."[2]   In attempting to meet this goal, the problem of racism in U.S. schools must be addressed. Because students of color are denied access to the benefits of public education due to institutionalized racism, they suffer the humiliation of higher detention and suspension rates (Fine, 1991). They are therefore regarded by many of their white counterparts as inferior, as "behavioral problems," or as underachievers. White students also suffer because these attitudes limit their own knowledge.

Racism does exist in American schools. The only question that remains is how to dismantle this institution. I found that one way to address this problem is to research and assess student views on racism (Donaldson, 1994). This research assists the antiracist/multicultural education reform movement presently taking place in this country. Student perceptions are critically important since their perceptions dictate their actions; yet their views have often been omitted from research studies and curriculum development (Seidman, 1991; Nieto, 1994a). It is essential to make all students aware of human equality and the benefits of diversity in order to guarantee a well-rounded education and greater success in today's society.

As an educator and researcher in the field of antiracist/multicultural education, I document in this book the racist experiences and antiracist solutions shared by numerous students from a variety of interviews, surveys, and study-projects. I am the principal investigator and antiracist education specialist for three of the studies that are presented: the High School Project, Middle School Arts Project, and Teacher Project.

Much of the book focuses on the High School Project, officially entitled "Racism in U.S. Schools: Assessing the Impact of an Antiracist/Multicultural Arts Curriculum on High School Students in a Peer Education Program" (Donaldson, 1994). Prior to the High School Project, which was based in an inner-city high school in a fairly large New England city, the school district, with a student population of 25,000, administered a student race relations survey with two thousand eighth- and eleventh-graders. Eighty-eight percent of student respondents agreed that racism existed in their school. As a follow-up to these results, the High School Project sought to explore and assess creative avenues that challenge racism in urban high schools. The project was established within the district at one racially and ethnically diverse high school through the development of an antiracist peer education curriculum model that used perspectives from multicultural education, the arts, and media. The major goal of this research was to discover, through the eyes of students, whether their learning, attitudes, and behavior were negatively affected by racism. Another goal was to demonstrate the significance of using multicultural arts and media to address racism in schools.

The Middle School Arts Project was used as a support study, to give additional validity for using the arts to address issues of racism for the High School Project. It focused on assessing an artistic fifth-grade social studies unit that infused the experiences of people of color during the Westward Movement. Finally, the Teacher Project, which evolved from student ideas for solutions, explored the antiracist education awareness of teachers from several regions of the United States.

Chapter 1 lays the foundation for understanding racism in society and how it is manifested in schools. In addition, it documents a number of efforts to reduce school racism. Through this review it should become evident that racism is pervasive and that not enough research, curriculum reform, or implementation is being done to address the growing problem of racism. As we acknowledge this dilemma, we focus on the significance of researching student points of view and ways in which they can become empowered to assist in the reduction of racism.

Much of the book is centered around using the arts within antiracist/multicultural education to address issues of racism in schools. Therefore, chapter 2 explores the interrelationship of the arts and multicultural education and how these combined disciplines can help reduce racism in schools and thereby enhance student learning and development. Chapters 3 through 5 weave student stories, ideas for solutions, and the High School Project into a comprehensive view of the perspectives of students on racism in schools. Because students in these various studies have identified many teachers as conduits of racism in schools, chapter 6 features a Teacher Project, an antiracist pilot study with teachers. Teachers in this particular study have participated in racism awareness surveys and in a student codeveloped antiracist curriculum model with implementation and evaluation components. In addition, this chapter concludes with recommendations based on research for the total school environment and gives suggestions for future research.

PREFERRED TERMS

Terminology used in the area of racism and multicultural education is constantly evolving. Words like *minority*, used to identify people of color, are now shunned by many because this term suggests a low status and falsifies global demographics. Many scientists and anthropologists tell us that terms used to denote race are scientifically incorrect. As they stand, *white, black, red, yellow,* and *brown* refer only to inanimate colors, not to human classification. Although many groups prefer to be called by their ethnic and national names, a difference of opinion exists in much of the research on racism.

Today, many people and organizations, such as the Institute for Healing Racism (Massachusetts), advocate that we are all one race, the human race. Although this is true, denying a person access to power and resources because of his or her ethnic background is a "norm" in the United States; racism exists widely.

My personal view is not to classify by color (i.e., white, black, and so on). When referring to non-European people, I use the term *people of color* as opposed to the term *minority*. Yet today even the term *people of color* is under great scrutiny. For many, it affirms solidarity between groups that are oppressed because of race (i.e., African American, Native American, Hispanic American, and Asian American), but many African Americans feel it is a repeat of being called "colored," which was a lowly term coined by European Americans. During my work as an antiracist education specialist, numerous European Americans have expressed dislike for the term *European* and have asked to be called *white* or just *American.* I always agree to call people what they want to be called, yet many times I point out that other groups in America usually do not get the privilege of being recognized as solely "American."

My goal is to be consistent and to identify each cultural group by their specific ethnic membership. For the purpose of this book, I have used terminology based on two additional criteria: (1) student-preferred terminology, that is, what students want to be called; and (2) the specifications of research documentation (for example, references to white and black will be used interchangeably with African American and European American according to the literature that is being cited).

Part I

SHALL WE SIT BY WHILE RACISM HURTS OUR CHILDREN?

Chapter 1

Racism in the United States and Its Schools

> Racism is present in so many ways in my school. For in-
> stance, teachers never say my name correctly, or they'll
> call me by other black students' names. It's embarrassing,
> and it hurts because they seem to know all of the white
> students' names.
>
> Interview: eighth-grader, Donaldson, 1995

RACISM IN SOCIETY

To understand how racism is manifested in schools today, it is important to begin with some contemporary views and a framework for understanding racism and the racist society in which we live. An equa-
tion that is helpful in this regard is "prejudice plus power" equals
racism (Pamphlet/Council on Interracial Books for Children).
Specifically, this means that the dominant group in power facilitates a
system of privileges and penalties based on race. In the case of the
United States, whites receive privileges, such as greater access to better housing, education, and employment; whereas people of color are
penalized and receive less access to the same resources. For example,
people of color are given less access to policy making and are excluded and marginalized in government, corporate business, education,
and all areas in which power can be executed. People of color are further subjected to white racist attitudes when attempting to attend white

schools, move into white neighborhoods, shop in white-owned stores, and so on (Tatum, 1987). Some macrocultural examples of racism around the country are as follows:

1. The 1986 Howard Beach (Queens, New York) incident where three African American males, stranded because of car problems in an all-white neighborhood, were attacked by a group of white youth. One of the victims was murdered.

2. In 1989 Yusuf Hawkins, an African American male, attempted to buy a car in an all-white neighborhood in Brooklyn. He was mobbed and beaten to death.

3. In 1992 Rodney King, an African American male, was beaten mercilessly with clubs by numerous police officers in Los Angeles.

4. These community incidents only reflect the institutional racism in our society. For example, while in office, President Ronald Reagan, in a speech before the International Association of Chiefs of Police, remarked, "It has occurred to me that the root causes of our . . . growth of government and the decay of the economy . . . can be traced to many sources of the crime problem. . . . Only our deep moral values and strong institutions can hold back that jungle and restrain the darker impulses of human nature." Most African Americans knew immediately to which "jungle" and "darker impulses" Reagan was referring, and that he was inciting white-against-black fear (Kromkowski, 1993). This type of government racist language also allows institutional racism to remain intact.

Institutional racism is also aided by the judicial system, which incarcerates a disproportionate number of minorities each year. Furthermore, the average sentence for a white inmate in 1986 was 112.4 months, compared to 149.6 months (an additional three years) for nonwhite inmates accused of similar crimes (Reiman, 1990, p. 100).

In 1995 numerous national racist incidents occurred. For example, in South Carolina Susan Smith killed her two sons and then claimed a black man had done it; Mark Fuhrman, a witness for the prosecution in the O. J. Simpson case and a Los Angeles police officer, perjured himself on the witness stand by denying that he had used the "N" word in the past ten years.

Racism: A Sick Belief System

Racism is justified through the mythical belief that the white race is superior to all races. It has been described by Pine and Hilliard (1990) as a "sick belief system" that is not a good match to meet the needs of all American citizens. Racism, as it is used here, is demonstrated at all levels of U.S. society. Currently, there is a great deal of debate over issues of racism in the United States. Numerous Americans, especially white Americans, insist that anyone can be racist (Stover, 1990). In this light, racism can occur when any person exercises prejudice or discrimination against someone else because of race. Yet many antiracist educators and other Americans, especially people of color, argue that it is impossible for persons of color to be racist because they lack the power to impose racism on white society. This definition reversal is often coined "blaming the victim," which means blaming people of color, the victims, for resisting or reacting to the racist oppression of the dominant society (Pharr, 1988; Pine & Hilliard, 1990). Antiracist educators suggest that, at best, people of color should be perceived as having racial prejudice as opposed to being racist (Adams, 1985; Hart & Lumsden, 1989; Mizell, 1992; Nieto, 1996; Pharr, 1988). Nevertheless, this does not mean that people of color cannot hurt others because of their prejudices.

It is important to analyze this "racism-can-be-practiced-by-anyone" concept and to understand who benefits from it, because this debate is causing much confusion with the younger generation. Traditionally, European Americans have benefited from oppressing people of color. In most cases, numerous forms of denial are used to cover up "white privilege" (McIntosh, 1988; Sleeter, 1994). When European Americans are allowed to point the finger of racism at others, they are able to hide their deep-rooted participation in it.

Research in the Branchard school system, which was the site for the study presented in this book, found that many young people did not fully comprehend the role of power in racism. They perceived racism simply as prejudice or hating someone because of race (Student Race Relations Survey, 1992). This partial understanding of racism can be detrimental because without clear insight into the role that power plays, it will be impossible for youth, our future leaders, to address and someday eradicate racism.

It is imperative that students understand that racism, as it is and has been practiced in the United States, is a fairly new phenomenon. It was developed by Europeans as justification to enslave and exploit people of color (Banks, 1991; Bennett, Jr., 1982; Garcia, 1991; Hamilton & Worswick, 1982b; Mizell, 1992). Nevertheless, although white society has initiated racist ideals, it is important to consider that not all whites are racists (Garcia, 1991). The understanding of these factors helps students realize that racism was created by humankind, and that not everyone is racist. Thus, the hope that racism can be eliminated is not inconceivable.

The ideology of racism is rooted in the belief of superiority and entitled privilege, and it has been passed down by white institutions from generation to generation. Although some whites suffer feelings of guilt, the material privileges are too great for them to give up (Adams, 1985). Therefore, many whites deny that racism exists or accuse others, as in the case of the "anyone-can-be-a-racist" philosophy; or they can place the blame on the victim. Those whites who take responsibility or refute the ideals of racism often become outcasts of their group (Tatum, 1993). These struggles and acts of avoidance allow racism to continue at full force in our educational institutions and in society as a whole.

Avoidance is possible when the definition of racism seems unclear. For example, when a person uses the term *white racism*, does this imply that there are parallel terms such as *black, brown,* or *yellow racism*? Many people are referring to *white racism* when they speak of racism in general. Yet others feel the term is necessary in order to delineate the role of European Americans in collectively oppressing people of color and controlling the wealth and power of the United States (Feagin & Vera, 1995; Sleeter, 1994). Because this issue is so complex it causes great confusion and therefore many choose to ignore it all together. In addition, racism is not static but changes from decade to decade, from the overtly racist Jim Crow laws of the 1800s and 1900s to the covert actions and racist code words ("midnight basketball," "welfare mothers," etc.) used by many politicians of the 1990s. How we attempt to recognize the many facets of racism today may not be true in the future. Yet, because racism harms so many Americans, we must do whatever is necessary to dismantle it.

Molnar (1989) suggests that white Americans assume that racism is something we "took care of" in the 1960s. Yet racism is still a serious problem today, although a different kind of problem than it was before the 1960s. The Civil Rights Amendment, which was passed in the 1960s, made it illegal to discriminate on the basis of race in employment, housing, and public accommodation, but institutional racism and individual racism still exist.

Both individual and institutional racism play major roles in the perpetuation of racism in schools today. Institutionalized and individual racism frequently overlap, but in order to explore how racism is manifested through each, we will look at them separately.

HOW IS RACISM MANIFESTED IN SCHOOLS TODAY?

Institutional Racism

Nieto (1996) states that "institutional racism is manifested through established laws, customs, and practices that reflect and produce racial inequalities in society" (p. 37). She also points out the importance of understanding the role that power plays in institutional racism. Those who are in power determine the policies and practices of institutions (Nieto, 1996). Pharr (1988) suggests that economic power has a strong influence on institutional racism. She asserts that "once economic control is in the hands of the few, all others can be controlled through limiting access to resources, limiting mobility, limiting employment options" (p. 54). There is a necessity to maintain racism and sexism so that people of color and women will continue to provide a large pool of unpaid or low-paid labor (Pharr, 1988; McCormick, 1994).

Institutional racism in schools flourishes through support at numerous levels of power (i.e., federal, state, and local). This power is reflected in entrenched policies and practices; biased curriculum; standardized testing; ability grouping; disproportionate rates of suspension, detention, and expulsion; and inadequate school funding. These areas traditionally benefit the white student population and victimize students of color. In addition, they are often camouflaged as positive policies and programs, and frequently students of color are blamed for the failure of schools to provide a means by which all students can succeed (Pine & Hilliard, 1990). It is very difficult for those who do not suffer such discrimination to understand the plight of the victims; therefore, institutional racism in schools is easily overlooked (Hart & Lumsden, 1989).

Ability Grouping and Tracking

The use of ability grouping and tracking in schools can make institutionalized racism apparent. Tracking is the practice of placing students in separate classes based on academic performance. Ability grouping, which often overlaps with tracking, is the dividing of academic subjects into different levels for students of different abilities (Oakes, 1986). Although these practices advocate that students work at their own intellectual pace, the measurement of intelligence is generally done by culturally biased, standardized tests (Medina & Neill, 1990). As a result of standardized tests and teacher decision making, high numbers of students of color are placed in low-ability and noncollege-bound tracks (Oakes, 1986; Wheelock, 1992). In addition, in her research Oakes found great discrepancies in student access to knowledge, instructional opportunities, and the classroom learning environments of higher and lower tracking groups (Oakes, 1986).

The curriculum does not necessarily help in this matter because it, too, can be biased. Nieto defines curriculum as "the organized environment for learning in a classroom and school. The curriculum includes both expressed elements (usually written down in the form of goals, objectives, lesson plans, and units and included in educational materials such as textbooks) and hidden elements (i.e., the unintended messages, both positive and negative, in the classroom and school environments)" (1996, p. 390).

In most cases, the curriculum that is used in schools today is monocultural, with superficial additives concerning other groups. Pine and Hilliard (1990) agree that the curriculum reinforces institutionalized racism by omitting the intellectual thought, scholarship, history, culture, contributions, and experiences of minority groups. They further suggest that the system prepares minority groups to fail while it prepares white students to succeed. Thus, white students are not required to be bicultural, bilingual, or bicognitive, whereas children of color have no choice. Yet, at the same time, these dual competencies and abilities are not validated as academic accomplishments.

In spite of the curriculum desegregation efforts of the 1970s to include racial minorities in lesson plans and textbooks, misrepresentations and distortions of minority groups persist (Gay, 1990; Grant & Sleeter, 1987). The efforts to examine and change discrepancies of class and gender in curriculum have been more visible than the addressing of discrepancies in how race is presented in the curriculum (McCarthy, 1988; McCormick, 1994).

School Financing

School financing is also inequitable. Students of color frequently attend schools that are poorly funded, with fewer resources and less qualified teachers than those of white students. Kozol (1991) cites many inequitable disparities in today's schools. He reports the average expenditure per pupil in the city of New York in 1987 as $5,500, while in the suburbs of New York funding levels rose above $11,000, with the highest districts in the state at $15,000. He further states that "New Jersey Courts noted that the highest spending districts have twice as many art, music, and foreign language teachers . . . fifty percent more nurses, school libraries, guidance counselors and psychologists . . . and sixty percent more personnel in school administration than the low spending districts" (p. 167). Although Kozol primarily focuses on discrimination based on social class, it is evident that racism is a factor in these inequities since children of color make up a large majority of the student population in inner-city schools. There is a strong link between classism and racism on both the institutional and individual levels.

Individual Racism

Individual racism in schools is often intertwined with, or supportive of, institutionalized racism. It rears its head through individual bigotry, racial slurs, graffiti, violence, and biased instruction. Nieto (1996) defines individual racism as "a personal belief that people of one group are inferior to people of another because of physical traits" (p. 22).

Throughout our nation, schools report racist acts (Murray & Clark, 1990; Stover, 1990). In most cases schools prefer to dismiss the severity of the problem by assuming that such incidents are isolated

(Hart & Lumsden, 1989). Yet thousands of students fail in school each year because of individual and institutionalized racism. According to Murray and Clark (1990), eight aspects of racism are common in schools at all grade levels:

1. Hostile and insensitive acts

2. Bias in the use of harsh sanctions

3. Bias in giving active attention to students

4. Bias in selection of curriculum materials

5. Inequality in the amount of instruction time

6. Biased attitudes toward students

7. Failure to hire racial minority teachers and other personnel at all levels

8. Denial of racist actions

Kendall (1996) recognizes that racism in schools today is much more subtle than in the past. Since it has become legally and socially unacceptable to support overt racism, it has been driven underground. For instance, teachers are now being encouraged to offer cross-cultural education in the classroom. Yet, because individual racist attitudes such as low student expectations remain the same, mixed messages are sent to the students. This can be as damaging as segregated education was before the 1960s (Kendall, 1996). One alarming statistic is that in spite of the changing racial makeup of students in public school systems throughout the United States, 87.2 percent of the teaching force is white (National Center for Education Statistics: 1990–91 SASS Report). Cushner, McClelland, and Safford (1992) describe this imbalance as a "clash of cultures" in which middle-class white teachers have difficulty relating to students with different backgrounds and cultures. It is therefore important to investigate the cultural baggage that many teachers bring with them into the classroom and its bearing on how racism is directly manifested in the school setting.

Many white Americans have been brought up with racist views that go beyond ethnocentrism, which is found in all human societies (Banks, 1991). According to van den Berghe, "there is no question that the desire to rationalize exploitation of non-European peoples fostered the elaboration of a complex ideology of paternalism and racism" (Banks, 1991, p. 75). Such ideologies were the basis for many European American biases, including that they have superior intelligence, culture, language, religion, behavior, and physical beauty. Media, which are controlled by the dominant group, have reinforced these values by characterizing "white as right" and all other groups as wrong or inferior (Citron, 1977). Often, because of white isolation from diverse groups, this myth goes unchallenged. The conflict arises when whites leave their families and communities for college or employment (Tatum, 1992). In many cases these institutions will be more diverse. The person who has no experience with diversity may feel lost or unable to communicate well with others from different backgrounds in the college or workplace setting.

With the changing demographics of the United States, whites are beginning to encounter more diversity. Such is the case for white teachers in the public school systems, but with one important difference. In most job settings, whites can interact with diverse groups on an adult level. In many circles today, we hear how getting to know a fellow worker of a different ethnic background enabled someone to dispel long-held stereotypical views. Yet, for teachers, the working hours are devoted predominantly to young people. During this time, teachers are the authority figures. They are given the opportunity to mold young people's minds, and often they do not consider the possibility of students educating them, or of learning about the cultures of their students.

Racist Attitudes of Teachers

Many white teachers assume that their ways of doing things are correct, thereby transferring their cultural values onto the students (Delpit, 1988; Pine & Hilliard, 1990). Students of color may experience this in the form of racist attitudes, as mentioned in the eight ways that racism is transmitted in the classroom (Murray & Clark, 1990). These racial attitudes often permeate the self-esteem of students of color. After their encounters with white ideology, many students begin to believe they aren't good enough or that they are inferior to whites. This teaching cycle has been around for decades, as many adults of color agree that they are still suffering from the effects of the disease of racist instruction. That is, they have internalized racism (Tatum, 1992). An example of this pervasive illness is reflected in a study that indicated that an African American teacher subjected African American students to ability grouping on the basis of family socioeconomic status and physical appearance. Thus, students with straight hair and lighter skin were more likely to be placed in the higher achievement groups (Rist, 1971).

Yet, more often than not, teachers of color are culturally sensitive to the needs of their students (Fine, 1991; Foster, 1993; Ladson-Billings, 1994). Before court-ordered desegregation, in the South black teachers were assigned only to black schools. They made a significant impact on the education of black youth. In a recent poll administered by a leading African American periodical, blacks questioned the wisdom of desegregation, because there has been no marked improvement in education for black children. The respondents of this survey also felt that black children were more likely to be neglected in public schools than white children because of the insensitivity of many white teachers and administrators (Foster, 1993).

It is likely that the public school teaching force will become even more white by the twenty-first century, at the same time as the student population becomes more diverse (National Center for Education Statistics, 1991). Numerous people of color have decided to leave or not pursue the teaching profession because of greater economic needs, teacher state competency testing that is biased, profound racist attitudes of fellow colleagues, and racist hiring practices (Fine, 1991; Pine & Hilliard, 1990; McCormick, 1986).

Pine and Hilliard point out multiple reasons why it is necessary to increase the pool of minority teachers: (1) it is an equity lesson for students, who must be taught respect for people from groups other than their own; (2) children of all ethnic groups must have access to diverse role models; (3) when a teaching staff is strongly skewed toward members of the majority group, the evaluation of performance is consistently (if subtly) biased against minority teachers; and (4) members of the majority group often misunderstand affirmative action and assume that those who benefit from it are less competent and less deserving (1990, p. 597).

In researching perceptions of racism among faculty in a New York City high school, Fine reported that "responses to the Teachers College (New York) survey reflected broad agreement that racism did not disrupt interactions among these high school faculty," but "a general critique from African-American educators across ranks revealed their sense of personal invisibility, alienation and being passed over for professional goodies. More devastating to them, however, was listening to colleagues disparage the students, local communities, and even some of the African-American staff in the system" (Fine, 1991, p. 150).

Racist Attitudes of Students

Racism is also manifested in schools through the attitudes of students. Traditionally, students of color have been the targets of racism. A 1989 study of hostility among racial groups in Los Angeles County found that African American and Latino students were much more likely than whites to be victims of racial slurs, name calling, assaults and physical violence, graffiti, and other forms of vandalism (Murray & Clark, 1990).

This resurgence of racist assaults can be attributed to several factors, including high unemployment, changing demographics, the influence of media with its emphasis on violence and stereotypes, and ingrained racist attitudes of family, communities, and institutions (Stover, 1990). White youth often reflect the racist sentiments of their families and communities. With the added pressure of job scarcity, peer pressure, and the threat of becoming a minority in the United States, whites have initiated racial attacks in schools, and these have risen throughout the country. In addition to white racial violence, interethnic hostility between the same racial groups (i.e., Japanese American and Korean American, West Indian-born and American-born blacks, Puerto Rican and Dominican students) is on the rise in U.S. school systems, as are incidents of hostility among groups of color (Stover, 1990).

The fact that often youngsters do not get to know one another as individuals can fuel racist attitudes in the classroom. Early childhood studies indicate youngsters are generally accepting of other cultures but as they get older and are more influenced by their surroundings, they become more reluctant to choose friends unlike themselves (Ramsey, 1987). If children are taught racist beliefs at home, segregated by ability groups in schools, limited by a monocultural curriculum, influenced by teachers' negative cultural assumptions, and subjected to racist peer pressure, then racist attitudes and behaviors are inevitable. An example of how students become provoked is a comment made by one of the students featured in the High School Project. She says, "Our classes are segregated. The kids of different races make this choice themselves, sometimes because of peer pressure to sit with one's own kind. The bad thing is the teacher accepts our division and goes on to teach the white side of the classroom first, then comes to give the students of color the leftovers. This makes me so angry, I want to hurt those white kids for getting special privileges."

ADDRESSING THE DILEMMA OF RACISM IN SCHOOLS

A review of racism in U.S. schools reveals that racism exists and more must be done to address and reduce systematic and individual racist practices in our schools. Antiracist educators share ideas on what needs to be done and some approaches to it, but cohesive followthrough between our nation's schools and government is lacking.

Hildalgo, McDowell, and Siddle (1992) suggest that our society has not accepted responsibility for the pervasiveness of racism. In addition, the general silence surrounding racism has enabled the U.S. government to chisel away at the accomplishments of the civil rights era. The researchers point out that in spite of the efforts to reform education, we are doomed to failure by ignoring the racial diversity of our country and our schools (Hildalgo, McDowell, & Siddle, 1992). Since both national and local interests affect the current state of affairs in public schools, it is essential to review both arenas.

At the national level, our educational institutions are still following the Reagan administration's "New Federalism" policies, which removed much of the power from the U.S. Department of Education and transferred it to local state and city education departments. No longer can debates on pressing issues of political and social change be discussed at the federal level, where press and public can monitor, mobilize, and organize for national solutions to national problems. "New Federalism" gave the power and funding, such as block grants accompanied by budget reductions, to local districts. At the local level, attention and mobilization are fragmented (*Readings on Equal Education*, 1986). Most public schools in the United States depend for their initial funding on local property taxes. The tax depends on the taxable value of homes and industries and is counted as a tax deduction by the federal government. Homeowners in wealthy suburbs get back a substantial portion of the money that they spend to fund their children's schools. This is effectively a federal subsidy for an unequal education (Kozol, 1991). This kind of unequal education helps ignite the rise of racism and violence in the schools.

At the local level, the situation is also problematic. Most U.S. schools have not been mandated by their local school boards to provide antiracist/multicultural curriculum.[1] In addition, schools and school systems generally do not seek antiracist/multicultural curriculum reform or programming until racist incidents have occurred (Donaldson, 1993a; Hart & Lumsden, 1989). Often, schools and school systems will seek the bare minimum, such as an in-service teacher workshop on civility or a "diversity day" for students. These actions are often prompted by the fear of lawsuits. Therefore, when the threat has passed, the diversity focus ends. Generally, school systems that experience repeated public racial incidents or have a large nonwhite student population opt for a greater degree of diversity curriculum reform. In most cases, addressing racism in schools directly is avoided, as is evident in the omission of such topics in textbooks, lessons, and school policy.

Many school committee boards and superintendents do not represent a balanced distribution of people of color (Pine & Hilliard, 1990); only 12.3 percent of public school principals are people of color (National Center for Education Statistics, 1991). This imbalance can lead to insensitivity to racism. Yet it is within the power of school committees, superintendents, and principals to call for educational summits, order surveys and studies, set policy, allocate funding, and formulate local and national support networks to help alleviate racial incidents within schools. Unless communities pressure school officials, antiracist efforts are seldom made. The major agents for change have been antiracist educators, community leaders, and grassroots organizations. The following section discusses some efforts that support antiracist/multicultural curricula, which can help foster positive change.

Local Efforts

In attempting to address racist incidents, several school systems have devised their own curricula, such as the Oregon School Study

Council (Hart & Lumsden, 1989). This antiracist curriculum encompasses a wide range of activities and policies. Two interesting incidents that developed as a result of this curriculum merit mention. Students at a Eugene, Oregon middle school were asked to write about their reactions to recent racial incidents in the schools. This assignment moved the students to take action against racism in the schools and community. One student shared his essay at a community assembly. Following his speech, he pointed out that he was wearing a rainbow ribbon, which symbolized that he wanted to live in an antiracist community. He then asked people in the audience to join his effort and wear a ribbon to show *their* support of a nonracist community.

In the second incident, Bahati Ansari, formerly on the staff of Clergy and Laity Concerned of Lane County, Oregon, contributed the idea of having a *racism-free zone*. This came about after her daughter suffered numerous subtle incidents of racism in a middle school classroom. Ansari borrowed the concept from Eugene's declaration of a *nuclear-free zone*. Here again, students took action. At the Spencer Butte Middle School, representatives from each class were chosen to form a committee. This committee met several times and composed a statement that was ratified by the student body, inscribed on a large plaque, and hung in the front lobby of the school. It reads:

Racism-Free Zone

> We will not make statements or symbols
> indicating racial prejudice.
> Freedom of speech does not extend to hurting others.
> We will not judge people by racial stereotypes.
> Racism will not be tolerated
> and action will be taken to ensure this.
> People of every race, creed, and color
> will be treated equally and are welcome here.

Spencer Butte Middle School declared itself a *racism-free zone* on April 13, 1988.

Antiracist/multicultural education after-school and activity-period programs also assist in reducing and addressing racism in schools. The Cultural Identity Group Project in Western Massachusetts is one such program. The project is a collaboration between the University of Massachusetts and the Fort River Elementary School in Amherst, Massachusetts. The goal of the project is to provide young people with an opportunity to explore issues of race and racial identity. The philosophy of the project is that by providing young people with an opportunity to voice their opinions of racism they will become empowered to address issues as they arise. Phase I of the project focuses on "affinity" groups, that is, students grouped by the same race. In these groups, students develop a greater appreciation for their own cultural, racial/ethnic group. Phase II focuses on "blended" groups; that is, groups of students from several racial and ethnic backgrounds. In this phase students from diverse ethnic and racial backgrounds develop skills to stop acts of racism and discrimination. Students and group facilitators meet for forty-five minutes weekly during lunch and recess. This project is currently being developed to serve as a model for other schools nationwide (Brown, 1995).

In 1994, when I took a position at Iowa State University, my concern as a parent was whether my children would feel safe and secure in their schools. My concern was amplified following several racial incidents involving racist epithets and graffiti experienced by one of my children while at school. To address this issue I offered to develop a multicultural club for students.

The Ames Middle School Multicultural Club is a before-school and after-school program in Ames, Iowa. The club is open to all students, and seeks to educate participants on multicultural issues and to empower students to address and share their knowledge with their peers. Each year students participate in a series of workshops that include, but are not limited to, understanding issues of racism, sexism, classism, and linguicism, as well as learning about numerous ethnic groups' traditions and experiences. With this knowledge, students have created a multicultural education club demonstration video to be used by their teachers and others in a general classroom setting. The participants also visit other schools in the district to talk about the club and how to initiate multicultural clubs throughout the schools in Ames (Donaldson & Visani, 1995).

The previous examples show that through the efforts of professionals, parents, and students, antiracist/multicultural education can be developed and practiced. (National efforts are highlighted in appendix C.) If all schools were to reform their curriculum to reflect such development, reducing racism in schools could become a reality.

Many ways to address racism in schools through the arts within multicultural education are also taking shape. For over twenty years, I have used the medium of art, specifically the visual and performing arts, to address sensitive topics. The following chapter gives an overview of the role of the arts within antiracist/multicultural education through highlighting the interrelationship among the arts, multicultural education, and student learning and development. I integrated these disciplines to conduct the research in the High School Project, which is discussed in chapter 3.

Chapter 2

The Role of the Arts in Antiracist/ Multicultural Education

> I think the arts are a good way to address issues because
> it's more appealing and attractive than just the regular
> desk and book thing that you do, just sitting in a class lis-
> tening to a teacher and writing papers.
>
> > Interview: eleventh-grader, Donaldson, 1993

THE INTERRELATIONSHIP BETWEEN THE ARTS AND MULTICULTURAL EDUCATION

The arts are a core component of multicultural education because throughout the history of human existence, culture and experience have remained alive in "the bosom" of the arts. Multicultural education seeks to explore and understand the experiences, lifestyles, and contributions of all the world's people. Therefore, the cultural arts cannot be omitted from the curriculum. Because multicultural education also seeks to provide an equitable education for all U.S. students, the development of diverse teaching strategies for the classroom is necessary (McCormick, 1984). Interdisciplinary creative and cultural arts are multisensory strategies that address the sundry learning styles and intelligences of all students (Gardner, 1983).

The advantages of having the arts as a core component of multicultural education have not yet been fully realized, in spite of the efforts of art educators in curriculum reform movements. Numerous art educators have attempted to infuse multicultural art education into the art classroom. The United States Society for Education Through Art (USSEA), founded in 1977, is a group of art educators who share an interest in multicultural and cross-cultural concerns relevant to the field of art education (Lovano-Kerr & Zimmerman, 1977, pp. 34–37; Wasson, Stuhr, & Petrovich-Mwaniki, 1990, pp. 234–46).

Art disciplines and individual educators have also addressed multicultural arts in general education (Daniel, 1990, p. 33). In addition, isolated programs and school systems have adopted multicultural arts into the total curriculum.[1] However, there is no national consensus or cohesive movement in education to solicit the integration of the arts into the multicultural education agenda.

To situate the place of the arts in a multicultural perspective, it is necessary to review the major concepts and curricular foundations of multicultural education. This section highlights definitions of both multicultural education and the arts. Following these definitions the connection between multicultural education and the arts is made in order to explain the importance of the arts within antiracist/multicultural education.

I begin with a discussion of multicultural education and a rationale for it. By exploring concepts of multicultural education, a contextual framework for the role of the arts can then be formulated.

Multicultural Education

Banks describes multicultural education as a reform movement designed to bring about educational equity for all students, including those from different "races," ethnic groups, social classes, exceptionalities, and sexual orientations (Banks, 1992, p. 21). Nieto similarly defines multicultural education as a process of comprehensive and basic education for all students that uses critical pedagogy as its underlying philosophy and focuses on knowledge, reflection, and action as the basis for social change (Nieto, 1996, p. 307).

Fundamental concepts of multicultural education in the United States are that education concerning many world cultures is basic education; that is, it is part of the core curriculum. Furthermore, curricula need to address inclusion of all cultures. Multicultural education addresses diverse perspectives, learning and teaching styles, teaching strategies, and pedagogical and sociological issues. According to

Gibson (1976, pp. 7–18), a multicultural curriculum is one that develops competencies in "multiple systems of standards for perceiving, evaluating, believing, and doing."

Multicultural education curriculum has been evolving for the past twenty years or more. The term *multicultural education* began to gain currency during the civil rights movement. At its conception multicultural education concentrated on issues of racism in education (Grant & Sleeter, 1987). At the helm of multicultural education development are pioneers, most of whom are established educators and academics.[2] They have gravitated to their ultimate goal of fusing the many perspectives, contributions, and learning styles of our pluralistic society into basic curricula. Through this effort, the definition and content of multicultural education have developed.

Although antiracism is still an important aspect of multicultural education, the wide spectrum of inclusion of other elements of diversity sometimes dilutes the efforts of multicultural education as antiracist education. An example of this would be how numerous schools choose to focus only on the celebration of diversity and not the "uncomfortable" issue of racism.

In spite of the evolution of defining multicultural education over the past twenty years, the majority of multicultural education textbooks used today seldom mention the significance of the arts in multicultural education or provide a definition of the arts. Although Nieto refers to the arts when describing the Eurocentric view of basic education, we are still left without a definition and clear connection of the arts to the goals of multicultural education.[3]

The Arts

Art is a skill acquired by experience or study in a branch of the humanities, or the product of such talent and knowledge. It is comprised of natural talent, but is also part of a way of life for numerous cultures. The arts, as interpreted through the Western view, are categorized as: "fine arts," which encompass the visual arts (such as painting, sculpture, ceramics, drawing, crafts, and multimedia); performing arts (drama, dance, music, and storytelling); and language arts (prose, poetry, and creative writing). The aesthetic experience is the inner-personal and inherent intelligence one uses when appreciating or producing an art form (Visual and Performing Arts Curriculum

Framework and Criteria Committee, 1982). When I define the arts, I speak about the aesthetic experience, the beauty produced by art and imagination.

Though not always acknowledged, the arts are an implicit component of the multicultural education framework. In the classroom where multicultural education is implemented, the arts can bring to life many ethnic and/or cultural experiences. Three concrete examples will illustrate this. Howard Rosenburg, an associate professor of art education at the University of Nevada, teaches a course on popular film and multicultural education. After taking this course, one student remarked that the opportunities to learn about other cultures such as African American, Native American, Hispanic American, and Asian American were magnified many times when films were used because they brought to the screen visions of real-life experiences. Rosenburg concludes, "While cognitive learning is enhanced by film, affective learning is, to a much larger extent than many of us care to believe, created by film" (Rosenburg, 1979, p. 13).

Dance, drama, music, and storytelling can bring to life immediately the experiences and contributions of dozens of cultures. Daniel, a dance anthropologist, tells us that "ethnic dance, like folk dance, is dance 'of the people'; it is explicitly connected to the sociocultural traditions of the group. It carries a history often retold in dance drama and depicted in ritualistic traditions" (Daniel, 1984, p. 14).

Keil, an ethnomusicologist, suggests ways "that music-dance and music-dance education might shape consciousness toward an agenda of world peace and justice" (Keil, 1985, p. 27). He proposes a full curriculum of Latin music-dance in our schools: "Latin music-dance, because it is at the center of Afro-European hybrid vigor, is the proper vehicle for creating such an *ethos*. Once established, this character-shaping music-dance praxis will give students a desire for all the world's musics and a much deeper curiosity about the world in general—its history, geography, cultures, and languages" (Keil, 1985, p. 80).

The arts can address a variety of issues in unique ways (e.g., racism, sexism, age discrimination, violence, drug addiction, parenting, etc.), and can develop other important skills such as critical thinking and leadership ability. Critical thinking helps students discover various points of view, examine issues, and draw conclusions for themselves. This promotes their sense of value as young citizens and ultimately develops leadership qualities. Students often begin to take an active role in world issues when critical thinking is incorporated in the classroom. Banks (1991) refers to social action as the highest level in multicultural education curricula. The arts within multicultural education can achieve that level; they are a proactive teaching tool that reaches into the personalities and intellect of students, and motivates them to take action on social issues (Rubin & Ruffin, 1993, pp. 39–42).

To understand the vast possibilities of combining the arts and antiracist/multicultural education to educate students, further examination of how these disciplines affect student learning and development is now shared.

HOW THE ARTS WITHIN MULTICULTURAL EDUCATION ADDRESS THE LEARNING AND DEVELOPMENT OF STUDENTS

Multiple Intelligences

During the 1980s work was done on redefining and reconceptualizing intelligence. Howard Gardner has been in the forefront of this development. According to him, "a human intellectual competence must entail a set of skills of problem solving—enabling the individual *to resolve genuine problems or difficulties* that he or she encounters and, when appropriate, to create an effective product—and must also entail the potential for *finding or creating problems*—thereby laying the groundwork for the acquisition of new knowledge" (Gardner, 1983, p. 61).

Gardner proposes that intelligence should be seen as a potential. He suggests that there are at least seven types of intelligence: linguistic, spatial, musical, logical, kinesthetic, interpersonal, and intrapersonal. These intelligences vary from person to person, and can be influenced by sociocultural factors, but none should be considered as better than another. In fact, he theorizes that possession of numerous intelligences enables greater total achievement. In the past, our educational institutions have based education standards and curricula almost solely on the logical-analytical intelligence, and many students who possess different intelligences have been classified as low achievers with less intelligence. This is especially true for students who are culturally different from the majority.

Some researchers have suggested that intelligence is itself a cultural concept, because a person who is able to function exceptionally well in his or her environment is intelligent. This measure of intelligence would differ according to location and culture, as in "the East's" acknowledgment of the introspective intellect and "the West's" adorning of the ability to deal with the abstract (Educators' Handbook, 1987).

The role of the arts in multicultural education can be viewed as a missing link among multicultural education, multiple intelligences, and learning styles. It is an integral piece that bridges the use of additional learning styles and intelligences in the classroom. This factor is important with regard to multicultural education, which argues that equal educational opportunity needs to be enhanced for students to exercise and explore their varied learning processes. Through Gardner's research, various intelligences are beginning to be acknowledged in the classroom, and the advantages of using multiple teaching strategies to reach all students are being recognized.

The arts engage most of the intelligences mentioned by Gardner, such as the linguistic abilities of poets and writers, the interpersonal (communication) skills of actors on stage, and the intrapersonal aesthetics of the arts as a whole. The arts also utilize visual (spatial), aural (musical), tactile (touch), and kinesthetic (physical) intelligences, which contribute importantly to integrating the learning process (Arts Framework, 1982). Within the arts we use many of the intelligences simultaneously. In fact, Gardner (1983) concludes that no performance (interdisciplinary arts) can come about simply through the exercise of a single intelligence. The enrichment of the intelligences of all students through the use of the arts is outstanding; this also can be said for student learning styles. Although learning style is different from intelligence, the two go hand in hand with regard to student educational development.

Learning Styles

Nieto defines learning style as "the way in which individuals receive and process information" (Nieto, 1996, p. 139). Bennett tells us that learning style is an emerging concept in education, and understanding that students have varied learning styles has become one of the most promising avenues for improved schooling. According to her, learning style is a combination of heredity and environment (Bennett, 1990). McCormick (1994) points out that learning styles is an equity issue, in that success in schools is linked with the analytical and linear way of thought opposed to other styles of learning. While learning styles reveal differing ways of learning among people of various cultures, Nieto (1996) warns that oversimplification can be dangerous; that is, teachers are susceptible to overgeneralizing learning styles of students on the basis of being educated on how various ethnic groups learn best. Generalization can lead to detrimental assumptions such as "race determines intelligence."

Understanding pitfalls such as these, the arts in multicultural education begins with an awareness of possible learning differences among people from different cultures, such as the analytic style characteristic of many white students, the more relational style of many students of color (Hesler, 1987, p. 6), as well as individual learning preferences, but focuses on sharing learning variations in the whole classroom setting. Most students seem to like the use of varied teaching methods in the classroom. Using the arts to learn multicultural concepts, many students feel excited about learning. But these opportunities are being missed because curriculum ideas in this area are still fragmented. That is, multicultural art education and art in multicultural education are often seen as different subjects.

Many art educators are beginning to recognize the importance of including multicultural approaches in their curriculum. Through the development of six position statements for teaching art in the multicultural classroom Wasson, Stuhr, and Petrovich-Mwaniki sought to assist art educators in recognizing and respecting the sociocultural diversity that may be present in their classrooms by designing and implementing culturally responsive art curricula. These position statements follow the guidelines of multicultural education as interpreted by such educators as Banks (1991), Chinn and Gollnick (1994), and Sleeter (1991).

Most of the multicultural arts research suggests that art educators must become knowledgeable in socioanthropological art studies. This means focusing on knowledge of the makers of art, as well as the sociocultural context in which art is produced (Wasson, Stuhr, & Petrovich-Mwaniki, 1992). The arts in multicultural education, on the other hand, advocate that general classroom teachers are able to use the creative arts in teaching multicultural/basic curricula (Daniel, 1990, pp. 20–22). However, numerous artists who support the arts within multicultural education debate whether general classroom teachers can provide this instruction. They feel that traditional artists must directly visit classrooms in person to share these traditional aspects of multicultural education.[4] In order to fulfill the learning aspirations of students, both the artist and general classroom teacher should be utilized. Developing the skills of nonartist teachers and continuously contracting visiting artists will help overcome such educational conflicts in the classroom. Yet these assets are often overlooked by schools seeking to infuse multicultural arts education into the curriculum.

Studies in Antiracist/Multicultural Art Education

Recent studies of arts curricula have demonstrated high student interest and motivation to learn in the classroom setting (Donaldson, 1993b; Gardner, 1993; Rubin & Ruffin, 1993). According to Rubin and Ruffin, theater enriches multicultural curriculum and impacts students' cognitive and affective abilities. An example they give is the play *Tribe,* which is about three Native American Indian tribes, their way of life, and removal from their original homelands to reservations by white society. After viewing this play, student audiences were moved emotionally, gaining a deeper understanding as well as being stimulated to think about the reality of Native American situations (Rubin & Ruffin, 1993).

Although not specifically related to the arts within multicultural education, the Arts PROPEL project is a curricular approach to art administered in a multicultural setting that directly assesses students' artistic learning. The project was developed collaboratively by the Arts and Humanities Division of the Rockefeller Foundation, Harvard Project Zero (codirected by psychologist Howard Gardner), the Educational Testing Services, and the Pittsburgh public schools. Its goal is to devise a set of assessment instruments that can document artistic learning during later elementary and high school years. This is done by using curriculum modules in conjunction with a processfolio that encompasses ongoing works and journal entries of students. The study modules encompass lessons in creative writing, music, and visual arts. Students and teachers document production, reflection, perception, and approaches to the lessons. Within each artistic component students have recorded significant growth. The results of this project prompted *Newsweek* magazine to select PROPEL as one of the "model" educational programs in the United States. Students and teachers in the project praised the curriculum and assessment method used (Gardner, 1993).

The Middle School Arts Project is also an example of arts curricula having a positive effect on student learning. After administering this social studies/multicultural arts program with nine fifth-grade classrooms, post surveys revealed that 97 percent of the students desired such programming in their classrooms on an ongoing basis. They considered the arts within multicultural education "fun," and could therefore remember the lessons better. They also felt they learned more from being able to receive and communicate information in a variety of ways. Regardless of cultural background, student participants enjoyed the mediums of dance, music, and drama (Donaldson, 1993).

Programming

A number of positive programs in multicultural arts education have been organized. These include Curriculum for Restructuring Education and New Teaching Strategies (CURRENTS) in New Mexico. CURRENTS' objectives are to ensure that multicultural arts and humanities serve as a basis for both teacher enhancement and systemic change in restructuring elementary and secondary schools throughout New Mexico, reflecting the rich and multifaceted heritage of the state. Inhabiting Other Lives, a program in the Dade County school system in Florida, is seeking to design a multicultural arts curriculum that will help overcome racial and ethnic barriers and conflict among students.

Although antiracist arts programming is considered multicultural arts programming, it uses the direct approach to the specific social problem of racism. At present, there is a need to formally include antiracist arts programming and other social/political arts curricula in the multicultural education/multicultural arts agenda, because it is often excluded from school systems attempting to infuse multicultural education in the curriculum.

Various antiracist arts programs have been developed at local levels such as the "Rock Against Racism" program developed in Boston during the 1980s desegregation turbulence. This group wrote and sang rap songs within the schools, addressing issues of racism. But as incidents quieted, the funding dried up and the program eventually died out. This is the case with many antiracist art programs. Within school systems, the value of the arts to address social and political issues has not been recognized. Instead, the arts are seldom utilized in the general classroom to teach about or counter oppression issues. Much of this is due to the evasiveness of addressing such issues as racism in schools, coupled with the lack of knowledge and respect of the arts for its teaching capabilities in all areas of education, and in particular, its special contributions to multicultural education.

Several antiracist/multicultural arts curricula have been noted by Rubin and Ruffin (1993). These include A. Nadine Burkes' efforts to study racism through poetry, in which teachers use drama to address both the racist and the victim, helping students gain insight and understanding. Jenoure suggests that "using social and political themes through the arts may help students to clarify their cultural definitions, identities, and purposes" (1993, p. 22).

Concluding Thoughts

Because the arts are inseparable from culture as a whole, multicultural arts education must be acknowledged as a viable part of the curricula and philosophy of multicultural education. As the nation's schools begin to develop curricula for multicultural education, the arts can take a prominent role in establishing a formal partnership with the schools.

In reviewing how antiracist/multicultural arts curricula benefits the learning and development of students, it is apparent that using the arts to teach antiracist/multicultural education has great potential to motivate the growth and development of students. Yet it is also evident that further programming needs to be developed, support solicited, and research studies carried out to develop the wide potential of the arts as antiracist/multicultural education.

Part II

STUDENTS TAKE A SOCIAL ACTION APPROACH AGAINST RACISM IN SCHOOLS

Chapter 3

Assessing the Impact of
an Antiracist/Multicultural Arts
Curriculum

> By participating in this project I now know that I have a
> voice and my voice is important. It is important for me to
> educate youth, especially the younger ones because we are
> the future and for racism to end we have to start some-
> where.
>
> Interview: eleventh-grader, Donaldson, 1993

In this chapter, the purpose and design of the High School Project that
is the focus of this book is reviewed. The setting in which the research
took place is first described to give readers a context for understanding
the study. In addition, the social context of the study highlights various incidents and substudies that took place in the school system and
prompted the project. In this study I sought to answer the following research questions:

1. How do students perceive racism and its effects on their learning
    and behavioral development?

2. Can multicultural arts curricula empower students to address racism
    in U.S. schools?

The purpose of the High School Project was to explore and assess
creative avenues of challenging racism in one urban high school

through the development of an antiracist peer education curriculum model that utilized perspectives from multicultural education, the arts, and media. The importance of this research is twofold: it fills a void in understanding the success of student-designed curricula and students' views on racism and multicultural education and the arts; and it opens the way for further development in these areas.

SETTING AND SOCIAL CONTEXT

The Branchard school system (pseudonym) is a large urban school system in New England with a student population of 25,000. The ethnic breakdown of the student population is 37 percent European American, 33 percent African American, 28 percent Hispanic American, and 2 percent Asian American and other. This breakdown is also representative of the city's residents.

The project that is the subject of this chapter was an antiracist education course and production for high school students interested in formulating a performance peer education group. It was accepted by the Branchard school department and administered at the high school. The project was encouraged by the school department because of the racial tension occurring within the overall school system.

As with many school systems today, the Branchard school system encountered media exposure for numerous racist incidents such as students of color being disproportionately suspended from school and the lack of people of color in administrative positions. In one specific incident at Branchard High School, which has a heterogeneous student population of two thousand, a teacher wrote disparaging comments about the lack of ability, sexual promiscuity, and violent behavior of students of color.

The community and the school department rose to address these racial problems. Although Branchard High School is ethnically diverse, its residents live basically in cultural-specific neighborhoods. In spite of this segregation, through the efforts of community organizations and the school department, an educational summit was sponsored. Approximately eight hundred people from all sectors of the community attended to voice their concerns about racism in the schools.

Following the summit, the Branchard school department issued a race relations survey to over two thousand eighth- and eleventh-grade students throughout the system for the purpose of assessing students' perceptions of racism in the schools. Questions focused on race relations with teachers, administrators, and other students, as well as on curriculum and school policies. There were significant differences for school, race, and grade. Two schools in the district perceived a significantly greater level of racism than other schools; blacks and Asians perceived a significantly greater level of racism than other groups in the system; and senior high students perceived a significantly higher level of racism than middle school students.

This survey supported the perceptions of students that racism exists in their schools. The results of these data determined the need for further investigation and follow-up. In addition, during this same time, I was administering a Middle School Arts Project to help combat the racism and violence occurring within the school system. Through this program, multicultural arts were infused into the social studies unit of nine fifth-grade classrooms in the Branchard school system. One hundred and seventy-three students and their teachers involved in this project were given preliminary and post surveys to determine their perceptions of racism and multicultural arts education. Out of this number, 168 students said they would like to have multicultural arts education included on an ongoing basis in regular subjects (appendix B).

The Middle School Arts Project gave additional evidence that many students are interested in multicultural arts curriculum. Specifically, the fifth-grade study helped address how antiracist/multicultural arts can help students become empowered through multicultural arts activities, one of the central concerns of the study reported here.

Following the summit and surveys, community and school ad hoc committees were formulated to make recommendations for school improvement. One of these suggested that "a task force of secondary students be established to address issues of racism and culture via training in areas such as bias awareness and communication skills. The students would study racism, multicultural understanding and sensitivity, and student-student, student-staff, student-community relations"(Student Race Relations Survey, 1992). It was in response to this recommendation that the High School Project was developed.

Having worked with the task force and on other projects for the school system, I approached the deputy school superintendent to ask him to allow me to develop an antiracist/multicultural arts project at the high school and he consented. This school had been widely exposed by the media for the racist incidents taking place there. Numerous newscasts featured Branchard High School students voicing distress over such issues at their school. This was an opportune time to get the students involved in a social action project to address the issue of racism in schools.

After receiving the consent of the school department I met with the principal, who also agreed, and she directed me to the peer education leader. The students in the peer education program designed events on social issues both in and out of school. The peer education group consisted of eighty students who met during activity periods. During the school year they had guest speakers and projects on AIDS awareness. Students would learn all aspects of AIDS awareness and then go with the program director to present this topic at other schools. In keeping with the thrust of the High School Project, the participants also dialogued and performed for others.

This study highlights the racism experiences of successful students to demonstrate that racism is not a figment of the imagination or a crutch that so many educators believe is typical of failing students. Another advantage of working with these academically successful students was that they were accustomed to taking on leadership roles in school. Yet the actual reason why I researched successful students in this study was because students who were failing their classes were denied access to extracurricular activities such as the antiracist project.

The students enrolled in the peer education program had outstanding leadership skills. They voted to take part in the antiracist/multicultural arts project in order to give all students the opportunity to address the issue of racism. They created audition posters and put them up throughout the school. Numerous students came to the auditions, but the core of the cast were members of the peer education group.

STUDENT-DESIGNED CURRICULUM MODEL

Without students, it would not be necessary to have educational institutions. Therefore students are the most important element of any school. According to Seidman (1991), there is a great deal of research on schooling in the United States; yet little of it is based on studies involving the perspectives of students. In order to analyze the problems of racism in U.S. schools and to develop antiracist curriculum, it was imperative to gather the views and experiences of the students. The design of the study project enabled this to take place.

The participants of the project created a problem-solving model/play entitled "Let's Stop Racism in Our Schools," which was performed at Branchard High School twice and at a racially troubled suburban middle school.

In response to the racial problems of the Branchard school system, the project sought to provide racism prevention programs on all levels. A study-project such as this was well needed, because it not only covered the system goal for programming, but it was capable of reaching out to the majority of schools in the system. One of the goals of the study was to encourage as many schools as possible within the system to begin racism prevention support groups of their own. One of the main objectives for the project was to expose selected students to utilizing the arts to teach with a multicultural perspective, and in particular, to address issues of racism. The objective was also to enable students to create their own performance model using various antiracism models as guides, and to formulate a peer education group that could perform for other students throughout the system.

Students attempted to meet these objectives through intensive sessions in the arts, problem solving, and multicultural education, under my guidance. This was achieved through the project's coursework.

A description of the actual coursework follows.

PROJECT ANNOUNCEMENT

The project was announced at the high school through handout and posted announcement fliers. A ten-week course commenced in 1993. Students met two days a week for classes and then for rehearsals. I visited the high school and spoke with interested students about the project. The first class was scheduled as a participatory drama, dance, and music workshop. It demonstrated one aspect of how racism began in the United States (i.e., through a reenactment of the forced migration to America and chattel slavery of African people). The purpose of the workshop was to illuminate the roots of racism in the United States and to display the significance of the arts in teaching multicultural education. Following the workshop, forty-two interested students signed up for auditions in a number of areas: creative writing; video production; music; dance; drama; graphic arts; and artistic directing and stage management. The interested students represented a variety of cultures. Auditioning students also stated why they were interested in participating in an antiracism project. Most had direct or indirect experiences with racism, or were interested in doing activities using the arts.

THE PROJECT

Following the auditions, twenty students were selected to participate in the project on the basis of talent and commitment. Classes met twice a week during a fifty-minute activity period. Because additional time was needed, after-school meetings were scheduled twice a week from 2:30 P.M. to 4:00 P.M. During the first four weeks of the project, the classes focused on learning about racism and students shared their experiences of racism. These experiences were integrated into the "antiracist/multicultural education" script, which was based on teaching others about racism. The goal of creating the script was to present the problem, the historical background, and suggestions for solutions. The script was open-ended in that it allowed for further discussion between cast members and their audiences. Students developed the script based on what they learned and shared during the coursework.

My role in this development was as an artistic producer/arranger and project director/educational facilitator. I made sure the script had continuity and was feasible for production. I encouraged the student writers to include all of the important points made by the cast members. In addition, I encouraged the group to include educational entertainment such as African dancing to portray the kidnapping of Africans to America, step dancing, poetry for the protest march, and a theme song about the tragedies of racism. I stressed to the students that if the play was both educational and entertaining to the audience, in most cases, they would retain much more of the information.

The final six weeks of the course focused on production: rehearsals, performances, and evaluation. Students did a total of three performances during this time period. These included: (1) a "work-in-progress" showing for teachers, administrators, parents, and community leaders in order to receive input on further development; (2) a performance for middle school students in another town; and (3) a performance at the high school for fellow students.

PRODUCTION ARRANGEMENT/PERFORMANCES

The production arrangement/performances began with script writing. Assigned student writers recorded minutes from each class; participants' ideas and experiences were creatively condensed into script form of approximately twenty to twenty-five minutes. Considering that school periods are traditionally fifty minutes long, the timing of the script performance allowed for a thirty-minute discussion between the audience and performers. This dialogue was as important as the script.

I was given the script draft for final editing; once approved by the participants, casting took place. After the "showing," the script was revised based on the performers and triangulator's (more will be said about the triangulator further on) video analysis, and feedback from the audience.

The arrangement for rehearsal and performances began with participants memorizing their parts. Rehearsals then followed a sequential pattern according to the student-designed script of four acts: (1) the protest march; (2) students' expressions; (3) roots of racism; and (4) students' solutions for reducing racism. In addition, students practiced articulating their responses to audience questions and comments. This was done through mock sessions that I administered.

After the "showing," students memorized the revised script and rehearsed for the middle school performance. In order to prepare for the final performance, minor revisions were made according to the middle school teacher survey evaluations, audience discussion, and participant recommendation.

Curricular materials used for the project included the course text *Think about Racism* (Mizell, 1992) and articles donated by the Healing Racism Institute and a multicultural education course. Regular videotaping was also a part of the curriculum, giving the students the opportunity to critique themselves on an ongoing basis.

All responses were grouped into two categories, which were consistent with my main research questions: antiracist/multicultural arts; and perceptions of racism with regard to student learning and development. In analyzing these data, common themes surfaced as sample models for schools interested in doing similar antiracist curriculum. Greater value and appreciation of multicultural education, the arts, and media may also emerge for educators reviewing the findings and analysis of this study.

Qualitative interviews with students were the heart of the data. Although the original intent of the study was to interview the students individually, I chose to comply with the students' request to have focus group interviews instead. I deduced that, since much of the project was centered around group discussion and team effort, it was acceptable to grant their group interview request. The focus group interviews ranged from two to eight students interviewed at any one time and were arranged according to the students' availability. These interviews lasted approximately one to one and a half hours. They were recorded on audiotape cassette and transcribed for research purposes. On the audiotapes and in the other documented data, students remained anonymous. They expressed their personal views of racism in the schools and whether this curriculum empowered them to do something about it.

The participant interviews were the central focus for analyzing the study. The interviews were guided by (but not limited to) fourteen questions (appendix A.2). Fictitious names were created for each participant and individual profiles were compiled from the interviews and field notes. Of twenty original participants, fourteen completed the interviews. Because of the small number of students and the group interview process used, I decided to develop an overview profile for each student. Each of these profiles is included in the next chapter.

A significant measurement component of the project study data was the project journal. During each meeting with students, I made an entry in the project log journal. The journal highlighted student participation, including discussions, problems, and activities accomplished for that day. I used it as an instrument to measure students' ongoing interest levels and progress in learning more about racism. In addition, attendance, scheduling, and planning were documented in the journal. I found it necessary to use the journal because only one qualitative interview was scheduled with each student. The journal was also used to record comments made by audiences after performances. This method reinforced the audience evaluation survey because many teachers and students did not participate in that survey.

In addition, observations from the projects' adult evaluators (social studies curriculum director, deputy superintendent, school principal, peer education leader, and triangulator) were documented in the journal.

The students' participation in the project was documented not only in text but on video- and audiocassette for further analysis. The value of documenting such data on video is great. For those who are sighted, it is estimated that 80 percent of human learning is done through visual contact (Wyman, 1991). With this in mind, a videotape of the "showing," the peer performance, and demonstration tape, without a live audience, was used as a learning tool for project participants. The students were able to assess their performance and audience responses by critiquing these videotapes. Their analysis was recorded on audiocassette tape and included each student's profile.

Prior to the student interview sessions, two videos of the production were shown: the June 1 peer performance and the demonstration performance. Audience evaluations were also administered and collected for the study. Two methods were used. The first was a five-question survey including information on ethnic background, gender, and status (work or school) for obtaining demographic data (appendix A.4). This survey reinforced the question-and-answer period following each performance. It gave students and teachers who were unable to speak during the discussion the opportunity to share their opinions.

In particular, all teachers who attended student performances were asked to complete the evaluations for the purpose of documenting teacher support. In addition, the "peer performance" student audience was given the surveys.

The second method of evaluation consisted of the verbal responses of the audience that took place directly following each performance. The general sentiments of the audiences were recorded in the project journal.

The project participants performed three productions. The first two performances only sought to distribute surveys to adults in attendance such as teachers, administrators, parents, and community members, for the purpose of identifying teacher/adult multicultural art curriculum support.

The third performance was in front of their peers. Approximately five hundred eleventh-grade students attended. Each student was given an evaluation survey prior to performance. Following the performance only forty-seven students had completed the survey.

These data assisted in the comparative analysis in determining teacher and student interest in using antiracist/multicultural arts curriculum to address racism in the schools.

SUMMARY

This chapter has detailed the study in terms of its research design, methodology, and data components for the purpose of presenting a model that can be used in any high school. The methodology, which used such diverse approaches as qualitative interviewing, quantitative surveys, evaluation, field notes, and video, ensured the probability of discerning students' perceptions concerning the effects of learning problems due to racism, and whether students can become empowered to address such issues through the arts.

The methodology consisted of a variety of approaches to address the creative nature of the research project and to analyze the interdisciplinary arts used in the project.

Qualitative interviews with the students were also conducted. The flexibility of this process allowed for individual self-expression and introspection. A trusting relationship between the interviewer and students developed the opportunities for students to tell "their stories." It is the heartfelt story that makes the most permanent impression.

The students were grateful to be given the opportunity to address the issue of racism in schools. They were excited to codesign curricula that could be used as a prototype for any school interested in incorporating antiracist/multicultural education into curriculum. They attended the course with great enthusiasm, read the required text from cover to cover, got their parents and community involved, and organized their own presentations. Those teachers and administrators who were able to see beyond the fear of confronting racism head on were amazed at the students' commitment level and their ability to develop curriculum and to articulate so well during antiracist discussions.

The students stated that they feel more motivated in regards to school when they are involved with real-life situations. This project demonstrated how teachers can use "real" curricula to make learning much more exciting.

The next chapter introduces the project participants/students through profiles developed from the group interviews in their own words.

Chapter 4

We Can Make a Difference

I think students' voices should be heard because sometimes students have good ideas.
                    Interview: tenth-grader, Donaldson, 1993

One major emphasis of this book is understanding racism in schools
through the students' point of view. This is important if we are to
grasp the problems they face in school as well as their abilities to address the problems themselves. The participants in these profiles
named themselves SARIS, so that all would know who they are.

Specifically, these profiles focus on the students' personal experiences with racism in school and how, as participants of an an-
tiracist/multicultural arts project, they were able to develop leadership
skills that promote the reduction of racism in their school. The student
profiles integrate excerpts from the student interviews and research
field/journal notes that I gathered (see qualitative interviews, p. 52).

During the interviews, students responded primarily to the research questions (appendix A.2). My interview data and field notes
help introduce each of the student profiles. Students' ages, ethnicity,
and participation in the development of the script are also included.

A majority of the students are African American (eight out of
fourteen) because during the auditions more African American students attended than any other ethnic group in the school. This cor-
roborates, in part, the findings from the Branchard schools' Student
Race Relations Survey (June 1993) that African American students

perceived the highest rates of racism in school. This result is supported by other studies that reveal that African American students perceive racism and are traditionally the major targets of it (Murray & Clark, 1990). In light of these facts, it is important to further explore students' views, especially those of African Americans, to find out whether antiracist curriculum can empower them to address such issues.

MARION

Marion is a Trinidadian American. She was seventeen years old at the time of the interview. Marion got involved with the project out of a deep concern for addressing issues of racism because she had numerous experiences with racism in school. There was one in particular that we used in the play. Marion had been placed in a special needs class and kept there for half the year before her teachers realized she belonged in regular college preparation classes. The school had assumed because of her accent that she was a special needs student. They did not give her any testing to find out otherwise. The following is an account of Marion's sentiments about the project and experiences with racism in school.

Racism has affected me at school in the following way. Last year I had a little incident with history classes. I wasn't learning anything about *me*. It made me feel very discouraged. I didn't have the urge to go to classes. I didn't have the urge to go to school. I just felt I wasn't learning anything about myself, so therefore I was not important. It can do that to you if you're not a strong person. It can make you feel very discouraged. Also, when teachers do not allow you to participate sometimes in classes, it really makes you feel you're not very important, and you don't have a part to do with the learning process. Like in my algebra class, the teacher has the tendency of teaching the white side first and then teaching the minority side afterwards. That makes you feel like you're getting the leftovers, second best or whatever. Yes, it has a very discouraging effect.

With racism, so far I find that I am a very angry individual. I think it is because of racism and how it has affected me. But I'm learning how to deal with it. I think through my anger I have become a much stronger individual and therefore I can deal with more situations.

I felt very empowered [participating in this project] and I still do. I was very discouraged, a little at the end [lack of moral support from their school] but now I know I have a voice and my voice is important. Therefore I can continue and carry on with educating people and letting them know. It is important for me to educate the youth, especially the younger ones because we are the future and for racism to end we have to start somewhere. The younger ones, like the kids in the suburban middle school [where they performed], are eager to learn. I think they're not faced with as much stuff as the older kids are, they just love everybody. If we start educating them sooner, when they get older they'll know that these things are wrong. Yet and still, I think that we should pay attention to the youth because they also have a voice. If we educate them and let them know that their voices are important and that races are not a bad thing, it will be a very strong position.

I have leadership skills and I think the whole experience here has strengthened them. Before I was really shy but now I can go out there and say what I have to say because I have a voice and it should be heard. I was educated a lot about racism but this whole experience has perked me up. It's given me a little in-step, like how to deal with it and respond to it. It has made me a more developed person all around than before.

I think the arts are important because people are more interested in real-life stuff, like the racism thing. Things that are real seem appealing to the youth because it's real. The kids are tired of seeing this fake stuff and this whole fake thing that's going on. People want to see the real stuff so that they can deal with it. If it is real to them they'll be able to understand it.

I've learned that racism is indeed a problem but that people are willing to come together to deal with it and that races can come together and work to improve a situation and make things better because in our cast we had Hispanics, whites and blacks and everybody worked nicely together. I've learned that people are just people. The whole experience was a powerful thing and that we can take a lot of positive steps.

Next time I think we should have smaller audiences because I think they kind of feel embarrassed to respond sometimes. If we concentrate on them they'll be more eager. As for the teachers, a lot of them are afraid of the subject, or they do not know anything about the subject. Guilt has a big part to play with it too. I would think if you educate them and say this is everyone's problem not just your problem, they may accept what we are trying to do.

RAMON

Ramon often refers to himself as "Spanish." He was seventeen years old at the time of the interview. Ramon was very enthusiastic about the project because he had been in several plays and was interested in continuing his dramatic pursuits. In addition to his dramatic interests, he was enthusiastic about participating because he had experienced several racist incidents and he was committed to trying to reduce racism in the schools. One of his experiences was shared in the play. In his own words in the play, he says:

As I entered my new class the teacher automatically stopped me and asked if I was in the right class. As I looked around and saw that I was the only Spanish person there, it dawned on me that she thought I should not have been placed in an advanced class. Once I showed her my class schedule, she then asked if I'm sure I want to be there. I answered yes, and then she warned me not to get out of line while in her class. A few weeks later she came up to me and said, "You're not what I expected, you're a good kid." Why is it that I was prejudged by my race to begin with?

Racism and how it affects me is not only with the teachers; it is with the students too. I remember when I was in CP (college preparation) classes and I was the only Spanish kid in there, and I used to be real good at math but all the other kids were white and I had just moved from an all-Spanish neighborhood and they didn't like me in that class. Because I was Spanish everybody used to ask me about Spanish questions. I learned more Spanish in math than I did math. I didn't learn no math at all.

I've got friends now (after being in this play). Well, I've got some friends I can depend on. I've got like a bigger family. I know I can go to Mohammad and Mohammad can come to me, or if I have a problem I can go to somebody. I'm not alone anymore. I have a more positive attitude. I can walk down the hallway with my head held high and no one will bother me because I have friends.

I really enjoyed working with this play. I was in other plays but we never went out to other schools. They didn't really give me what I wanted. When we started this play I really liked it. I stuck with it. I feel it benefited quite a lot of people out there. I think we are helping some students because there are some students that have come up to me and asked me about what I was doing and what I was trying to say. I explained it to them and some people walked

away like, "Na, it's always gonna be like that," but other people were interested and wanted to become a part of what I was doing. I think we touched
some people but we can't please everybody.

JESSICA

Jessica identifies herself as white American. She was fifteen
years old at the time of the interview. Jessica came to the project later
than the others, by way of Ramon. Her main interest in the beginning
was to act. She had been in several plays prior to this one and her
skills in acting were very honed. She received a crash course in
racism, memorized the revised script, and was on stage for the last performance which was done at Branchard High in front of their peers.
Her first experience of audience reception was painful because this
audience was very noisy and rude.

I never actually had a teacher who is racist. I mean, I never encountered any
teacher who was racist against anybody, that I know of. If one of my teachers
was racist, I'd be surprised. I don't think I have any of them that are. But I
think if I would encounter any teacher that was racist it would be hard on everybody in the class. It is hard for everybody to learn because everybody has
to work together to learn. It is not as easy if the teachers are trying to put
down certain people. In a class everybody is supposed to speak up, in a way.
Everybody should have discussions about what you are learning and if certain
people are left out, you don't really get as much out of the classes as you
should.

When you are reading a textbook most of what you learn is from the
white male point of view, and that's all you learn. That's some of the problem
why people are racist because they don't know about other cultures. I think
one of the ways to try to stop racism is through education, through people
learning about others. If you know more about others you won't really think
of them as different or that something is wrong with them. I think the more
people learn about others then the less people will feel that way.

I think that being in this play has helped me, number one, to realize how
much racism is out there, because I said before I was really surprised. I always knew that racism was a problem but seeing how people reacted to us
made me think a lot about how people feel about other people. A lot of people
are racist and it just surprised me, some of the people who are my friends that

reacted to what I did that way. This made me mad and this helps me learn about what other people think.

I think that the arts help to develop leadership roles because I think that people are most interested in the arts. You can see something, hear something and it makes more of a difference than just reading something or being told something. Also, the arts are a way to express yourself through music, writing, and acting, then just saying things. It's easier to express yourself in a different way and it helps because students are more apt to listen to things that they can feel, see, and listen to.

Students' voices should be heard because a lot of the problem does come from the students. Us students are thrown together every day for six periods a day. We have to learn how to work together or not work against each other. And to hear what people think helps to form your own views; also it helps for you to realize how people will actually think. I didn't know how a lot of people thought before this play. I think it is good to know what other people think.

The project is very needed in our school. So many people who I didn't think were racist actually are. I really didn't think there were that many people who felt that way in school. Maybe I'm being naive but I really didn't. I was scared after that performance. There were people saying that they were going to kill us and beat us up, and all sorts of other stuff. It was uncalled for, even if they didn't agree with us. I mean if I was listening to a group I would at least go in with an open mind about it. The audience was being very immature. It really made me mad and upset me a lot.

I am glad I got involved with this play because it gave me a chance to voice my opinion against something that I really believe needs addressing. I love the chance to get up and say my opinion whenever possible. It gave me a chance to do that and also gave me a chance to learn things that I did not learn before and meet people in the school that I didn't know before. It was a good experience and I feel that we have helped a few people out there and we have helped ourselves. I felt it was worthwhile. I'm going to be in this next year and the year after because I have two more years. I'm just going to stick with it because it's something I really believe in. Hopefully we can get more people to join us and try to influence people on the way they think.

MARCEL

Marcel chooses to be called African American. He was sixteen years old at the time of the interview. His favorite medium in the arts is music. He was a choir member both in and out of school. When he auditioned for the play, he was very bashful. Yet he was very motivated to combat the issue of racism in the schools.

Racism can affect my learning by many ways. I don't know if they are all obvious but to me they are. Like if I had a teacher who is racist, let's say against African Americans or blacks, and the teacher is trying to teach you something but they don't like a certain race people they wouldn't teach you everything. They would work with the other groups and you'll be left out a little bit. That's probably how come they say you're stupid. They should give you a free chance to learn and be equal with everyone else.

I want to say this play has helped me. It helped me become more familiar with the different forms of racism. I also thought and knew people were racist but not such a big group of them. Now I have a better understanding, and the book that we got that came with the play has helped me also. I've been doing a little research on that, so I'm getting a more ideal concept.

In my opinion I think that it would be easier if we had more curriculum, more school subjects with the arts because if people want to learn and do something they like to do, then they put all their effort into it. When people see people doing things with all their effort, they memorize it and they try and learn a lot from that. Instead of just reading it, like Jasmine said, you read the paper and you don't remember it all or you won't read it all. For me there are some things I like to do, when I do, I do them with all my heart. It's easier to perform or do it the way people are more comfortable with.

I think students' voices should be heard because regardless what people do, they do it around their friends because their friends are mostly students, and they each see a different pattern of something in them, for instance, racism. They can recognize this and talk about it.

I think now the majority of people at Branchard High School have seen what we're trying to do and what we're about. If there are any more talented people out there I hope they will be interested in joining the play so we can make it more worthwhile, more with the arts, more people can put their hearts into it, and more people can get a stronger message. In the future I would like to also represent peer educators in this play titled "Let's Stop Racism in Our Schools."

GINA

Gina, who is Puerto Rican, was seventeen years old at the time of the interview. She is a dedicated member of the peer education program. As a representative of this program she has attended AIDS and diversity conferences. Her devotion to help facilitate positive change led her to audition for the project. Gina had encountered several racist incidents in school, one of which was documented in the script. In the play she shares this experience:

Last year I was placed in an advanced class. While there, I had a low average because I didn't understand the work. My teacher told me that I would have to work twice as hard to get a good average so that I wouldn't turn out like all the other Puerto Rican girls who get pregnant by the age of sixteen.

Racism has affected me since I faced it in school in my classes and stuff. It's made me want to work harder to prove them wrong, prove all the stereotypes wrong, and just show them I'm not as they believe. I'm much more smarter and I can work just as hard as everyone else. It's made me a much stronger person because I can deal with a lot of things now. I can actually look at a person who just made a racist comment and not laugh, and tell them, "That was not right what you said." I feel like a better person about myself. This has given me a lot of confidence to go up there and say, "I prove you wrong," and "Ha, there!" I think that learning about racism and teaching other kids has inspired me. It's given me a lot of confidence. I can go and teach other kids about how racism hurts everybody. I feel I can make a difference wherever I go. I can go down south and make a difference, even in a very racist community. Just learning about it and seeing how a lot of people reacted toward our play, and the way we deal with racism has just given me a lot of power to do something about it.

I have developed a lot of leadership skills, even just speaking out to people. But dealing with racism I can actually tell my friends now, when they say a racist remark or they laugh at somebody because of anything. I can say, "You shouldn't be doing that, 'cause you don't like it when people do it to you." I've learned just how to be a leader in my community. I've made a lot of friends. I can just speak out and talk about things.

I think that the arts are powerful in developing leadership skills. Just because you feel comfortable when people will listen to you. If you see that they are listening to you, you feel comfortable going and talking to people. It's more appealing, of course. I'd rather sit and watch somebody perform than sit and listen to somebody talk. It gives you twice as much information, not just with what they say but what they do, their actions.

I think that I learned that using performing arts, it could be a song or a play or anything, is very helpful in teaching and educating other people. We use the same means at the peer institute and it really worked. The project was with people our own age, and they were more respectful of course. I learned a lot about racism, where it came from and how it hurts people. I just learned a lot. I met new students. I learned that everybody can work together and be happy. I would just like to add, from reading the textbook and having discussions I learned all the ism's, and when I went to the peer institute at the workshop on discrimination we had to list all the ism's and what we thought they meant. I think I took over the group. Everybody was just amazed that a teenager knew what the ism's were and what they meant, not what they put them out to be. A lot of times they sugarcoat things, we [she and Jimmy, another project participant] weren't sugarcoating it. I think I learned a lot from the book and the discussions.

DONNA

Donna calls herself African American. She was seventeen years old at the time of the interview. She is very active in cultural endeavors such as the African American Society Club at school. She is also on several sports teams at school and is very active in her community.

Racism has affected my learning a lot this year. Well, it's affected me all the time in school. But really it's just making me stronger because I have to try a little bit harder in my classes to get good grades to stay on the honor roll. It's really hard when your teachers tell you that you're not bright enough, you're not good enough or something. But I think it's because I've had a strong family background and therefore I was able to do everything good. But some students, they don't have anything to look forward to. They don't have anyone telling them what they should be doing, and when teachers say negative things to them they just give up, they drop out. Basically, racism has affected me by making me a little bit stronger though when somebody says something racist to me, at that moment it makes me very discouraged and angry but in the long run it makes me a stronger person. Not that I'm saying I like racism or that people should keep giving it to me so that I get stronger, I'm not saying that. Since I have gotten some racism it has made me a stronger person.

I just wanted to say that racism affects my learning on all different levels because I'm learning that adults are not all that they think they are. Some of them are not perfect people. We are taught that adults are always doing the right thing and by getting racism from my teachers, I'm learning that they are human too. They can be just as ignorant as young people can be and in some cases they are.

Yes, I did feel motivated to stop racism. At the beginning of the production I was feeling very powerful like I had a voice and that I could make a big difference, and I was really excited about it. But after performing for our peers I was more frustrated than anything else because during the course of the day people were coming up to me and making jokes. They were stepping, a dance I was involved in the play. It was good that they liked the step dance but the play wasn't about a step dance. It was about stopping racism and educating people and letting them know that racism is here. I was annoyed and frustrated that that's all they got out of it. Even some teachers, even my math teacher, she didn't know what the play was about. It was strange because she was a grown woman standing there listening. It wasn't really very hard. But when we performed for the suburban middle school I felt very excited about it because the kids were excited and they were really cute. They had good questions, that made me feel good. It made me feel very motivated to stop it. But when people have defeatist attitudes, and they're very negative and pessimistic about everything that makes it hard for me to go on doing this.

I think that before I got involved with this I had good leadership skills but I think doing this play and educating people has further developed my leadership skills.

I learned from doing this play that there are more kids out there that are a little more serious about life and serious about solving problems such as racism. It was a good experience for me. Also, I learned that racism is a much bigger problem than I thought from the beginning. There is a lot of ignorance out there. A lot of the ignorance is coming from adults. And it's really a lot of adults. When I say adults I'm speaking about the teachers. They just want to ignore it and think that it's going to go away by ignoring it. Some of them don't want to admit that it exists. Education is gonna get rid of the problem. I think that this is a good play. We need to keep doing it and keep trying to educate people. But I think a lot of people are too stuck in their ways to change right now. It is going to be hard but I think we should still try.

This project is to let everyone know how students feel about racism in schools. A good idea instead of asking teachers to come to see the play is arranging with the principal to maybe go into one of their faculty meetings.

Instead of performing the play just explain what the play is about. That we're against racism, we're not against teachers, white people, or any particular race. We're against racism and the problems that it causes in our schools. Teachers are afraid of the topic, afraid to address it, so instead of expecting them to come to us we should just go to them so that they can't have any arguments about it.

DARIA

Daria, who likes to be called either African American or black American, was sixteen years old at the time of the interview. Daria is very active in the peer education program. When given the opportunity to join an antiracist/multicultural arts project she leaped at the chance. She was very instrumental in developing the project script, and was willing to do anything to keep the project going (such as selling candy). During the project she was quite sickly and had numerous family problems, but this did not stop her from attending all meetings and performances. Daria had been very troubled by racism in her school and was committed to making a change.

Racism, ever since I was a child, has had a negative effect on me. It's always made me feel depressed and had a negative effect on my grades. I always did bad in my classes where I had teachers that were racist or that always put me down because of my color, well that's the same thing. Up until now, I didn't really know how to deal with the situation. I just kind of took it all in and didn't say anything about it. But now if somebody says something racist to me, I can respond in a positive way without getting upset about it or taking it to the point where it affects me and my grades or my attitudes or self-esteem.

Because racism has always affected me, I always felt I had to make a difference somehow, particularly with racism. I feel good about trying to do it. I think that by the theater and the arts I can help reduce racism.

Before I started this project I didn't really know too much about what racism was, except that it existed. I knew a little bit about it, that I guess it was whites against blacks, that's how I really thought about it. But I really learned a lot. I learned where it came from and the background and how people really feel about it, and how to deal with the situation when I am approached with it. It was a good experience.

I think the arts are a good way to address issues because it's more appealing and attractive than just the regular desk and book thing that you do, just sitting in a class listening to a teacher and writing papers. I think it put more fun into learning and more interest. It makes people want to learn more about their subjects and the arts.

JAMES

Because James felt he was such a mixture of ethnic backgrounds, including Italian, French, and Indian, he asked to be identified as just white American. James was eighteen years old at the time of the interview. Throughout the project, he worked after school. Very often he would rearrange his work schedule to make it to after-school rehearsals. During outside rehearsals or performances he always helped drive students without transportation. James was very dedicated, as were all the students, to the project. Yet he was the most quiet unless he really felt he had something very important to say.

I think that students' voices should be heard because sometimes we have good ideas and the teachers they either listen and don't do anything about it or they don't listen. If you did talk to them about what they could do, they probably wouldn't do anything about it.

I think that racism will affect us because we're the future. We right now are the future, our kids are probably gonna act the same if not more into it than we were. If it keeps going it's going to get deeper so we better slow it down now, for our kids and for us.

I don't think it [racism] has affected my learning in any way. Besides stopping class in the middle of classes because someone else called someone a name. We had to straighten it out before we could get back to class.

I remember one instance when I was taking a gym class. There was a white girl and a Puerto Rican girl, they were both pregnant. The gym teacher pushed the white girl as far as she could go and she babied the Puerto Rican person. She just like left her alone and let her do what she wanted to do. She made the white girl like get up when she was sitting down, she was never standing still at one time [to James, this was a racist reaction toward the white girl].

My definition of racism is me thinking I'm better than someone because they come from a different country, even though they were born in America, but their relatives come from another country. Instead of just saying I don't like them as a person, just because he's this race doesn't make him any different. To say that all people from one country must be alike, that's racism. I think that if one race thinks that this other race is going to keep "me" down then "I'm" going to keep this race over here down.

I think that the arts should be used more because it's not being used a lot. People just have assemblies but they're not using the arts. The arts can demonstrate how to solve a problem.

IRENE

Irene identified herself as African American. She was sixteen years old at the time of the interview. The cousin of the school deputy superintendent, she is quiet and a devout churchgoer and she delights in academic challenges. Irene took on the most difficult parts to memorize in the play.

Racism affects my learning because if I have the slightest feeling that a teacher is racist toward me, then you kind of work toward what the teacher expects of you. If a teacher is racist then they'll have low expectations of you, or just think certain thoughts about you because of the color of your skin. It will affect my learning because I won't try as hard as I would had if I thought the teacher had great expectations of me.

I'm glad I got involved with the racism play because it enabled me to get more knowledge about racism and to also make new friends.

I didn't know a lot of facts about racism, I've heard a lot of opinions. Through the book and the play I learned more facts about racism so that now when I say something about it, it won't just be opinion. Also, I learned that there are so many racist people who don't know they're racist. Because it's something that is taught, when you're taught something you just assume that's right. These people really need to be educated about it.

I think students' voices should be heard because, for one, students are constantly hearing it from older people. They are always hearing, "Do this, do that." They are constantly getting instructions on what's right and what's wrong. But when you see someone up there who is your age, who still has to be instructed by adults too, but they're giving their point of view and telling something, this kind of makes you listen because they're in the same league as you are. I think that it is important for us to talk to them [other youth] because it makes them at least listen a little.

Students get tired of sitting in a class and using a book, and then that same thing every day. You know when you go to school what you're going to do: you are going to have your book and sit down with your paper and write.

When people get into things like drama they're interested more, so they can have leadership skills. On top of that when you're watching something it makes you able to talk about it. When you're talking about it and you have everybody's attention and you're up there like we were up there in the play, you're in control at that moment. The more you do that the easier it becomes and you develop that skill of being in charge.

MOHAMMAD

Mohammad was born in Iran. He was seventeen years old at the time of the interview. Mohammad is a member of the Ba'hai faith. One of the core doctrines of this faith is to accept all races equally. Through this consciousness he became active with the Healing of Racism Institute and this project. Mohammad was also a member of the school's Honor Club Society. Although Mohammad felt he had never been discriminated against because of race or ethnicity, when he introduced himself at the beginning of the peer performance the audience roared with laughter because of his accent and Iranian last name.

Racism has affected my learning because sometimes in my class I see that one of my teachers are racist against one of the students, and you don't look up to that teacher anymore. You just can't take their word as truth anymore. But I personally haven't really faced racism, myself, here but in Iran I faced sort of, well not racism but prejudice. I was kicked out of school because of the religion I practiced; that is basically the same thing as racism here.

I knew about racism before I got involved with this play because I was involved with the Institute for the Healing of Racism. But what this play did for me was that it gave me the opportunity to get involved, to get more involved in reducing racism, which is really important.

I think students' voices should be heard because the class with different ideas results in the right answer, usually, most of the time. I think that the best way we can show leadership is by us practicing our antiracist views. By never saying any racial jokes and standing up for other people's rights that are of other races.

I'm really happy to have been involved in this play and grateful to Ms. Donaldson for helping us start an antiracist thing in our school. I just want us to have an antiracism support group, like an after-school curriculum thing.

NICKY

Nicky liked to be called African American. She was seventeen years old at the time of the interview. Nicky was inspired to join the project because of difficulties she was having in getting hired for a job, where there was a strong indication that she was being discriminated against because of her race. She applied for a youth job in which her application was lost and after reapplying she was told all positions were filled, but she knew of white youth that had gotten a job after she was denied.

During my life I have experienced exclusion that was racist. I felt that what was said to me was racist and should not have been said. As I am involved with a program that tries to reduce racism I've not only learned how to confront it but also from being educated and reading the textbook it gave me more knowledge of what is all about. I can help reduce it by just understanding the techniques of learning.

I learned about the history of racism. How it affects everyone as an individual. I feel this is a very good experience for me because it made me understand how to relate to this issue. It is very important for everyone to get involved to solve the problem. It would work if everyone worked as a coalition. They must seek this education if they want to be successful.

Since I have got myself involved in this performance, it has made me become more stronger and empowered. Because during the time I was experiencing racist exclusions. I learned through the performance what things are best to do and how to confront the problems that came about with me. I think that it was very important to go for whatever you want to seek, and to have ambition.

JIMMY

Jimmy calls himself African American. He was seventeen years old at the time of the interview. Jimmy is very community-conscious, as are his parents, aunt, and uncle. Although he was not interested in performing, he was very motivated to join the project because of its objectives; therefore, he auditioned to be the stage manager and set designer. In addition, Jimmy was very active in the AIDS prevention and diversity conference promoted by the Peer Education Program.

Overall, he was interested in helping make positive social changes in his community.

Racism in a way has affected my learning but then again it hasn't. It makes me a little bit smarter about what things are going on and how to deal with it. It hasn't because I haven't had any direct incident within any of my classes or with any of my teachers, yet.

I learned a lot from this whole thing, not only about racism but about how people react to it, and that it is something that is very strong and it's not easy to get rid of. It is something that we all have to come together and work at real hard or otherwise it isn't going to work. At the Peer Institute, the theme was celebrating differences, because this has a whole lot to do with the things that are coming up, that are happening, and things that have happened in the past. As far as the performance, I think it is better to perform in front of younger kids than older. A lot of older kids think they know everything. A younger kid is amazed, they say, "Oh shoot, I've never seen anything like this before," then you're happy about it. You don't get the kind of negative feedback that you do from your own generation.

In the beginning when this all started up, I thought I had a lot of power to do something very positive for me and for people in my generation, and I still do. When we performed for the suburban middle school it made me feel really good because of the kids. They look up to you as being someone positive, a positive role model. If they see you doing something they like, they go, "Hey, maybe I can do that or I can be like him or her." It's kind of hard sometimes when your peers are constantly putting you down or putting the things you do down. In your mind you always have to think that you still have the power to do anything you want and that if you want to make a difference you can no matter how hard it is or hard the obstacles are, they're always gonna be there and you just have to overcome them.

I think I've developed a lot of leadership skills through this project. Now I know a lot more things about racism. I can go home and tell my parents about it. If they ask me something about racism I can either tell them or get back to them. In a way I've kind of become a leader with my friends. The friends that are not always in the street. The ones that are with me chillin' and coolin'. If there is something they want to know about racism and I know it I can tell them, they think of me as a leader.

SHERRY

Sherry identifies herself as black American. Although she recognizes that her ancestors are from Africa, she feels she is not African so she prefers to be called black. Sherry was sixteen years old at the time of the interview. She, as many of the other participants, became motivated to join the project based upon the initial antiracist performing arts workshop. She enjoyed the reenactment of how racism came to be prominent in the United States and wanted to be part of a group that would educate others.

Racism has affected me in a couple of classes like my English class. I barely passed that class. Because my teacher will teach to one half of the class, and not really explain things. Like for me, the way she acts toward me, makes me really not get the stuff. Then I try to get extra help, because when she teaches the class she doesn't give her all because mostly everyone in the class is black or Hispanic; there were like one or two white people in there. I'm not trying to, you know [complain about the teacher], but that is how she would teach. One day I had a study and I took that study in her class and the majority of students in her class were white. I noticed she explained more. She gave her all. In my class when we would take her test, no one would pass but I noticed in the other classes they passed.

We should be concerned with the problem of racism because when we get older in life it's going to affect us greatly, even more than it's going to affect us now because we're gonna have to teach our kids that. For me, I know when I have children I know I'm going to teach them how racism is. I will teach them they shouldn't hold things against others because they are a different race. I will try to teach them the best way I can that they shouldn't grow up to be a racist person. Students that are younger than us are aware of their surroundings because it affects them every day because it's not like it was ten years ago, so I feel like if you're going to ask a student how they feel, you should try to get information from students of all age levels.

Through the arts I learned to better myself toward racist things, things that are prejudiced. Now I can teach other people not to be racist or prejudiced. I got to give my input and other people got a chance to know how I felt and they got to know my ideas.

JASMINE

Jasmine likes to be called African American. She was sixteen years old at the time of the interview. Jasmine enjoys singing and she helped coordinate and write the play's theme song. Often, Jasmine would be the peacekeeper between participants when a point may have been taken the wrong way. Her patience and humor were real assets to the project. Jasmine responded to the research questions in a very brief manner:

If I know a teacher is racist I wouldn't want to be in that class, I wouldn't do anything.

I read some of the responses on the audience evaluation sheets and there was a lot of racism on the sheets. Yes, they said they would protest with white hoods and they were using words like "nigger."

I feel I have a better understanding of racism and more knowledge. I know more about the history. I plan on going places and letting people know about this problem we're having. I feel that students should be heard because it shouldn't just come from an adult or parent point of view because nobody will get the full picture. We have to hear from both sides.

People prefer visual [media and the arts] than reading. Like they watch TV more than they read the newspaper. I think the arts can show them a way to express themselves in a more positive way.

CLOSING COMMENTS

Because they had spoken frequently in previous group discussions about private matters, the students felt free to express their views openly and honestly in the interviews. This cooperation aided the research immensely. Their responses demonstrate a broad range of experiences from student leaders in an urban heterogeneous high school.

Many of the students' responses correlated with the literature on students of color as targets of racism (Murray & Clark, 1990; Pine & Hilliard, 1990). Students were taught in a segregated manner, and students of color were given less teaching time than white students and were often negatively prejudged because of their race. Such racist acts did have an effect on participants' perceptions of their learning and development. This pertinent information from the students' point of view promises to add to "racism in schools" research. This information is invaluable when developing antiracist curricula for K–12 students.

Many remarked that the project had given them newfound knowledge to deal with racist situations. They also felt, through the project, that they had developed leadership skills to make others aware of racism in schools. Most agreed that the arts should be infused into basic subjects and that they had a way of conveying the "real-life stuff."

Chapter 5

Now That We Have a Voice, Who Is Willing to Listen?

The profiles documented that racism affected students' learning and behavioral development in three major ways: (1) by belittling their self-esteem, causing diminished interest in school; (2) by heightening students' perceived need to overachieve academically; or (3) by making them feel guilty and embarrassed at seeing other students victimized. In this chapter, these problems are further discussed, along with the findings concerning how the multicultural arts curriculum empowered the participants to address racism. Additional data, such as the audience evaluations, support surveys, and student video evaluations, are included in this analysis.

STUDENTS' PERCEPTIONS OF RACISM IN SCHOOL

The Effects of Racism on Students' Self-Esteem

Of the fourteen profiles, only the two white students in the study said they had never experienced racism at school directly. The students of color, on the other hand, perceived that racism damaged their self-esteem, and all but two students of color admitted to experiencing racism in their schools.

The students of color were very often resentful of unequal treatment and tended to internalize this mistreatment, either by withdrawing their interest in classes and/or feeling that they were not good enough in the eyes of the teachers. This was the case with Marion, who lost the urge to go to school because she was not learning anything about herself. She grew angry at the system and felt she must be second best because teachers would not allow her to participate in class or would ignore the students of color while teaching white students.

In cases where students of color had strong family support and a knowledge of their history, they were able to survive racism in school without as much damage to self-esteem as those who did not have similar support. Donna, for example, admitted that because of her strong family background she was able to achieve in spite of some of her teachers telling students they were not bright or good enough to succeed.

The African American and Hispanic students perceived racism to affect their learning and behavioral development in a number of ways. For example, they were not able to share or learn about their ethnic groups' contributions in the classroom. Many said they felt cheated and disrespected, because their cultural groups made major contributions to the United States but this was ignored. This curricular omission often resulted in their becoming disinterested in school, skipping classes, or distrusting adults and the curriculum, thereby not wanting to learn.

The participants mentioned these reactions numerous times while enrolled in the project. For example, in her interview Jasmine indicated that "If I know a teacher is racist I wouldn't want to be in that class, I wouldn't do anything." Respondents from the audience surveys made similar comments, including "If students are treated unfairly they will retaliate by not listening, doing work or skipping."[1]

Jessica, the white female participant, shared her frustration with both racist and sexist curricula during the interviews: "When you are reading a textbook, most of what you learn is from the white male point of view, and that's all you learn. That's some of the problem why people are racist because they don't know about other cultures."

The school curriculum is not generally representative of diverse cultures. This fact also made the students of color feel invisible, marginalized, and unimportant. The feeling of being "less than" was magnified in segregated classes in which teachers gave priority to white students. During a rehearsal, Sherry responded to this dilemma by mentioning that teachers' racial discrimination made her dislike white students and she would often start arguments with them (Field notes, May 18, 1993). This behavior was also a deterrent to student success in the classroom because frequently these students would be sent to the office and receive in-house suspensions.[2]

In response to these experiences with racism, students of color expressed feelings of low self-esteem, anger, and discouragement. Daria, for instance, indicated that racism made her feel depressed and had a negative effect on her grades. Another student remarked, "I find that I am a very angry individual. I think it is because of racism and how it has affected me." It appears that most students were emotionally traumatized because prior to the project, many did not have outlets in which to vent their disappointment and frustrations.

Students of color perceived racism to affect their overall well-being, education, and development. Although all harbored these sentiments, some consciously chose to rise above their dilemma and succeed in school. One biracial student from the audience survey defined this outlook by saying, "Racism affects learning to the degree of letting it affect you. You have to be strong and overcome these obstacles."[3] Many of the participants held this same view. For example, Gina responded to racist treatment by attempting to prove all of the stereotypes wrong: "I'm much smarter, and I can work just as hard as everyone else." The participants' peer leadership education and/or home support helped develop these attitudes. Yet even these students admitted that, at times, they doubted their value because of others' racist attitudes. The audience survey also reflected these concerns. One student stated, "If students are told that they aren't good enough, they'll think that way and won't try hard enough to get anywhere because they don't think they can."

The audience evaluations reinforce many self-esteem issues expressed by the participants. Some comments included: "If they're made to feel lower, they will not want an education"; "It's hard to learn if someone's always putting you down"; and "If you feel bad, your work will be bad."

Students most often enter school with positive self-esteem. Yet, through the examination of the participants' views, support data, and review of literature, the challenge of maintaining positive self-esteem in school because of racist attitudes and behaviors can become overwhelming for many students. The influence of racist experiences on the dropout rate of students of color is well documented (Fine, 1991; Clark, 1993; LeCompte & Dworkin, 1991). In addition, this study recognizes that many students who are expected to graduate from high school, such as the sample population of peer leaders, may carry the negative effects of racism over into their adult lives.

Achievement Motivation

Achievement motivation is defined as the need or concern for excellence (Wilson, 1987). All of the participants in the study felt the need to excel in school. The participants were peer leaders, and because of their membership in this group, they were required to do well in school. In spite of receiving passing grades, they experienced numerous conflicts in learning because of racism in school.

In most cases, these students referred to racist acts on the part of teachers and administrators rather than student-to-student prejudices. The participants mentioned on several occasions that they felt less intimidated by the racist attitudes of their peers. Most of the participants perceived that other students did not have the power to cause any real racial problems at school when there was a balance of white students and students of color. Comments such as, "They can say what they wanna, but they can't give you a grade," and "We all [student body] pretty much get along because we have an even mix," were mentioned (Field notes, March 25, 1993).

In response to their perceptions of adult racism, students mentioned being distrustful of teachers and administrators. While some students felt alienated from school, others opted to work relentlessly to prove their teachers' racist expectations wrong, either by disassociating with others or, as in Gina's case, working twice as hard. Some of the students tolerated teachers' racist attitudes to receive a passing grade. For example, Ramon allowed his teacher to prejudge his behavior on the basis of race because he wanted to remain in advanced classes.

Students often felt overwhelmed and unable to deal with racism. Many decided to bury their resentments deep within themselves because they felt their reports of racism would not be believed. This issue came up several times during discussions with participants (Field notes, April 6 & June 8, 1993).

In other cases students did exactly the opposite. By observing the participants' relationships with other students, I discovered a variety of ways that the students of color would mask their desire to succeed in school. Frequently, they would "clown around" or speak "hip talk" with their "homies" (friends), attempting to show that they were not "selling out" to the establishment. Many students of color, because of the fear of being seen as "acting white," which in this case means achieving and accepting monocultural curriculum, attempt to cover up their interest in such success when associating with their cultural group/peers.

This phenomenon was described in research by Fordham and Ogbu (1986). They researched black students' school success in an all-black high school in Washington, D.C. The researchers sought to understand how the fear of "acting white," manifested in such actions as speaking standard English or complying with Eurocentric school curricula, causes black students to sacrifice their academic achievement. The study found that the collective identity and "fictive kinship" of black Americans influenced their success, or lack of success, in school. Participants in the present study who achieved took on the same characteristics as those described by Fordham and Ogbu.

One difference between the studies was that the participants in this study often utilized their leadership skills to help other students overcome their skepticism of school success. Nonetheless, other students embarrassed them by calling them "butt-kissers" because of their grades and participation in academic extracurricular activities. An example of this is when the participants could not use the auditorium for rehearsal, and they had to rehearse in the cafeteria where other students were serving out their in-house suspensions. In the beginning, the participants refused to practice in front of their peers, but after I reminded them that they would be performing in front of them ultimately, they agreed. As they started to practice, most of the students on suspension moved forward to see what they were doing. At first these students laughed and "teased" their efforts, but after becoming fully aware of the content, they began to say words of encouragement to the participants. The more the participants felt empowered, the prouder they were to share their knowledge and achievements with others (Field notes, April 15, 1993). This incident demonstrates the ability of the participants to convince others that education and addressing issues in education were not bad aspirations.

Racism had an effect on students of color in the study with regard to achievement in school. It gave some the determination to achieve beyond what their teachers and peers expected. Yet instead of feeling successful, their accomplishments left a bitter aftertaste. As one student put it, "Racism makes me very discouraged and angry but in the long run it makes me a stronger person. Not that I'm saying I like racism or that people should keep giving it to me so that I get stronger, I'm not saying that." In the case of other students, they agreed with Ramon, who said, "We're passing our subjects but it hurts to have others racist toward you" (Field notes, March 25, 1993).

Guilt and Embarrassment of Seeing Other
Students Victimized

Although the white participants and the Iranian student did not perceive themselves to be targets of racism, they were also affected by it. Each student had different views but essentially they all felt guilty and embarrassed to see other students victimized by racism.

Mohammad, the Iranian student, stated that when his teachers were racist to other students, he couldn't look up to those teachers or trust their word as truth anymore, and that this had an effect on his learning. He responded to these injustices by taking a stand and joining the project.

James, one of the white students, was concerned about another white student who was the target of prejudicial treatment. He felt a moral obligation to stop the buck here and begin to make changes for future generations to live in greater harmony. He saw himself fulfilling this goal by participating in the antiracist arts project.

Jessica was surprised by the amount of racism that exists in schools. She was embarrassed by her friends' racist attitudes, and felt guilty by her association with them. During her interview, she made comments such as, "A lot of people are racist, and it just surprised me. Some of the people who are my friends reacted to what I did that way. This made me mad and this helps me learn about what other people think."

Tatum (1993) would describe Jessica as a white ally because she chose to deal with her guilt and embarrassment by doing something about it. She and James took action to help dismantle racism through participating in the project. Not many white students at the school were willing to take that risk.

In general, the participants were embarrassed and resented not having a multicultural curriculum in textbooks and lessons. They felt they were being deprived of a better education and that this omission very often diminished the cultural pride of various students. From group discussions, this general consensus was written in the script: *When I look through my American history book I feel cheated. I know that there were Americans of all colors that contributed to making America great but I don't see them in the book. This makes me feel like I'm not getting a full education. Stop racism in our schools.*

The Student Race Relations Survey highlighted this general consensus also. Almost all of the respondents saw few classroom activities that reflected multicultural contributions. Over half of the respondents offered no solution. Although over 10 percent said there was no solution, over one-third indicated that there was. They recommended teaching young children not to hate those from other races and cultures, including history about each different group in the curriculum, and having students produce a television program showing the evils of racism. Students suggested holding dialogues while blindfolded or having some students live with other racial or ethnic groups for a time. Some students thought an interracial team could be formed in each middle and high school to deal with racial or ethnic questions. Some suggested interracial "study buddies."[4]

Students in the project unanimously agreed that the antiracist/multicultural arts project empowered them in several ways to have a voice to address the issue of racism. They developed a sense of power through the interviews, performances, development of the curriculum/ script, and discussions with audiences, adults, and peers. They felt this was an ideal medium to reach out to others, especially youth. One of their major concerns was the future of today's youth.

The students felt the arts had the ability to relay the "real-life stuff" that youth must be made aware of in order to succeed in school. With the approach of student audiences asking the opinions of the participants, leadership roles were further developed.

Students also agreed that the arts should be integrated into basic subject areas. It was generally felt that utilizing the arts would make classwork more interesting and add to the cultural dimensions of learning. The participants made statements such as, "I think the arts help to develop leadership roles. You can see something, hear something and it makes more of a difference than just reading something or being told something"; "In my opinion I think that it would be easier if we had more curriculum, more school subjects with the arts because if people want to learn and do something they like to do, then they put all their effort into it."

The participants envisioned how the arts could encourage more participation and interaction, to the extent of collaboratively designing curricula that could address and engage students and teachers to produce social action activities in the classroom. Marion commented that "I think we should have smaller audiences because I think they kind of feel embarrassed to respond sometimes."

They felt empowered by being asked their ideas on and off stage. Donna said, "When we performed for the suburban middle school I felt very excited about it because the kids were excited and they were really cute. They had good questions. That made me feel good. It made me feel very motivated to stop it [racism]." And off stage Ramon said, "I explained it to them and some people walked away like 'Na, it's always gonna be like that,' but other people were interested and wanted to become a part of what I was doing" (Interview, June 19, 1993).

These responses were similar to those in the fifth-grade multicultural arts study. This program/survey supports the primary study with regard to the significance of using the arts within multicultural education to address issues and to become integrated as basic education. This program/survey as discussed earlier was implemented at the middle school level. It was infused into the fifth-grade social studies unit and reflected the perspectives of people of color, who are so often left out of school textbooks. The underlying objective was to foster cultural awareness and appreciation for both students and teachers, and to work with teachers in developing ongoing creative teaching strategies. Specifically, the program was designed within the "Westward Movement" unit. Two workshops, on Native American and African American contributions during the westward expansion, were presented for each fifth-grade class. Preliminary and post surveys were also done.

Students revealed many things they had learned, such as "I learned about my ancestors and I liked it"; "It helped me feel a little bit of what people felt"; "How different cultures helped to contribute to make America"; and "I learned more from people than the book."

One hundred and sixty-eight students said they were enthusiastic to have multicultural arts education again. The five students who said they would not like to have art workshops again were all males. One remarked the arts was "just not his thing" (appendix B).

In understanding the interest level of both primary and secondary level students, the participants' suggestions of concentrating their performances on the elementary/middle school students were appropriate. It was through their performance for the middle school that they felt the most satisfaction.

This performance was done at an almost all-white middle school of six hundred students. The cast received a standing ovation and numerous questions from the student audience, such as, "What should I do when my friend is calling other students racist names?" Donna replied, "Take a stand. Tell your friend you'll have no part in it."[5] One week after the performance, the cast was notified that the students at the middle school were still talking about the production, and the middle school audience all agreed that the group was courageous. Furthermore, the middle school students, because they were also young, could relate far better to the high school students than to adults telling them what was not right. The cast members were elated because of this performance and response. Marion said, "It is important for me to educate the youth, especially the younger ones because we are the future and for racism to stop, we have to start somewhere. The younger ones, like the suburban middle school, are eager to learn."

It was then they realized the potential of their efforts to reduce racism in schools. At the beginning of a subsequent rehearsal, the participants rushed in all together and very ecstatically shared their brainstorm idea for a name for their group. On that day, they decided to unite to form SARIS (Students against Racism in Schools).

This newfound sense of empowerment did not go unchallenged. On the day of their peer performance, elation turned into dismay. The school administrators did not notify teachers and students about the performance until two minutes before the bell, at which time they were only told to file into the auditorium. Teachers were upset because of the disruption of their class schedules. They stood on the sides and in the rear of the auditorium, away from their students. Of one principal and four assistant principals, no one came to the auditorium to announce the performance. Much of the student audience was loud and unruly throughout the performance, and those who tried to hear the show could not. This situation devastated the cast. Just before the performance opening, the cast member who was assigned to introduce the play was laughed at disrespectfully by the audience as he said his Iranian name. The cast, backstage waiting to go on, began to break down into tears. As they consoled one another, they insisted they had to go on to help dismantle some of the ignorance that was in the audience. They performed in full force regardless of the audience's laughter and remarks. Following their performance they took stage positions to answer questions from the audience. In spite of the poor auditory quality during the performance, the audience took turns coming to the microphone to ask questions and voice their opinions. The cast responded to these questions articulately, and the audience seemed to be very impressed. But when one audience member began to name teachers whom students perceived as racist the discussion began to get heated. Just as this began to happen the bell rang and students were asked to go to their next class. Many students from the audience became irate and demanded to have more discussion time.

Later that day, the principal asked the student who directly named racist teachers to make an apology on the school's cable station. The cast members claimed that this apology made the whole school think that the performance was both negative and racist—just the opposite of what it was intended to be.

After meeting and sharing their sentiments with one another, they decided to visit the principal's office. It was there that one of the assistant principals listened to their grievances, apologized, and promised to do it right the coming year. The cast was not satisfied. Yet, through it all, the participants discovered that their empowerment engendered both support and resistance. This acknowledgment solidified the need for their work and heightened their determination not to give up. They reflected on this experience after watching the peer performance videotape, and Marcel remarked that "Even though we had a lot of conflict, I think it was pretty good how we got everybody's opinion." Mohammad agreed that "It was really productive because everyone got their point across. The audience stated their opinions about what they thought. This really brought out the facts about racism." Ramon said, "I think this tape could be used in schools, to show how no one likes racism. That's why everyone was arguing and stuff." In response to this statement Irene said that "I think that the lack of teachers and administrators showed us what a sensitive topic it is because I think that it was not so much they couldn't come, it was that they didn't want to come. Because it is something that not many people want to talk about, including teachers, but of course they are people too" (Field notes/video critique session, June 19, 1993).

This dialogue indicated the depth of awareness the students had gained. They began to offer recommendations to make the play more successful. These included having a smaller group as an audience because it's easier to discuss sensitive topics like racism in a smaller group. The participants recommended that they should announce what the audience will see in the performance. As Jessica put it, "Prepare them, so that they don't have to walk in with a big chip on their shoulders." The students felt that if the audience was more aware of what they are doing they could avoid a lot of the turmoil that took place during the June 1 performance. In addition, the audience must be told what would not be appropriate in the discussion following the play, such as identifying teachers by name.

The third videotape was recorded without the presence of a live audience in hopes of using the tape as a demonstration tape for interested schools and classrooms. After viewing this tape Mohammad commented that "I think it was perfect. I think the teachers will really need to see these and use them in their classrooms. It will just bring out the fact that racism exists. Most teachers don't know that. They try to deny it, but this will help them bring it out" (Field notes/video critique session, June 19, 1993).

All the students were excited about the prospects of making the tape available to interested schools and teachers. They began to plan a time to present the tape to the school department, along with a copy of the script/curriculum to be used as a student-designed curriculum model in the system. But for initial feedback, the peer and demonstration videotapes were viewed by the peer education leader, the project triangulator (outside colleague), participants' parents, and outside teachers who had not attended any of the performances. The peer education leader stated that the students had accomplished their immediate goal of addressing racism in the schools through the medium of the arts within multicultural education. He agreed that more of an explanation of the group and the process would have to be shared with teachers and student audiences. This concern was also mentioned by the project triangulator. The parents, on the other hand, thought the participants were exceptional and demonstrated tremendous growth through their participation in the program.

The outside teachers, who viewed this tape at an in-service teacher workshop, were surprised by the students' perceptions. This stimulated dialogue about how racism is a major problem for many students in school. Overall, these teachers were willing to look at the points being made by students and help find solutions to the problem. They felt the video/performance was an excellent way of making people aware. Most said they would use this tape in their own classrooms.

All of these steps reflect the students' sense of empowerment and outreach through the multicultural arts project. This sense of empowerment fostered greater leadership skills and a personal outlet for the participants to overcome racial conflicts. The study also found that by enabling the participants to make new friends from a variety of backgrounds with an interest in antiracist curricula, a bond was established that gave the students an even greater sense of empowerment. Some examples of this would be Ramon's response, "I've got friends now. Well, I've got friends I can depend on. I've got like a bigger family." Irene shared similar feelings when she said, "I'm glad I got involved with the racism play because it enabled me to get more knowledge about racism and to also make new friends." Through this camaraderie the participants were able to face the school administration when it appeared that the school was nonsupportive.

The audience evaluations provided an added opportunity to explore what the audience deduced about the performance and the worthiness of multicultural arts curriculum. The first audience evaluation was administered at the first production, which was an in-house work-in-progress performance for teachers, administrators, parents, and interested community members. Out of the large teaching faculty, only three teachers attended and two were African American. After the performance, the cast spoke with the audience. Students wanted to know why the teachers did not come to support their efforts, but no clear explanation was evident. The African American teachers shared that students are not the only people who experience racist attitudes in schools. They suggested that teachers do also. They gave examples of white students not respecting teachers of color, and colleagues not wanting them to be a part of the faculty. Others from the community, such as the chairperson of the education committee for the NAACP, deputy school superintendent, peer education director, and community organizations (Healing Racism Institute) gave words of encouragement to the students, that in spite of the unpopularity of an antiracism production, they should continue to stand up and deliver the message that students and others need to hear.

Seventeen audience evaluations were completed at the "showing." Many of the evaluations suggested that the cast become more diverse. There was a general consensus that knowledge and programs such as this will help decrease racism. One parent remarked that the program would be great for the regular classroom. The audience felt that it might help the teachers not be as racist in the classroom and cause students to think differently. All of the respondents commented on the excellence of the performance and the courage of the cast.

Many of the thirty-three respondents said they would like to see multicultural arts curriculum developed for regular classroom use. Some of the direct responses to this point were: "It has the ability to get to the root of many problems that are troubling students in school," and "We need this type of influence in each and every school" (Audience Evaluation Survey, June 1993).

When asked, "What is your opinion of students assisting in the development of multicultural curriculum?" forty-one of the student audience respondents agreed that it is good for them to do so. Some of the direct responses to this question included: "These students should be allowed to develop school curriculum because they are very strong; they had the strength and courage to do this"; "They make me feel proud to know that they was doing something to help with the racism problem"; and "Students need to be more active in this movement" (Audience Evaluation Survey, June 1993).

In addition to the student audience evaluations, two teachers submitted evaluations on that day. One of the them was a fourth-grade teacher who came as a guest. She felt that this type of programming is needed to set the groundwork for learning about all people and that it should start at the elementary level. She also wrote: "I feel it is very important [students assisting in the development of multicultural curriculum], seeing that they will be our leaders in the future. They need to be involved, as soon as possible, in the direction their lives will move, and can move in."

The other teacher was a grade 10–12 teacher at Branchard High who was very disturbed by the performance. She felt that all teachers were being accused of being racist, and that this in itself was racist. She commented that "If you take people from all walks of life, I believe that you will find teachers in Branchard to be among the *least* racist of people. If we were, we would all go teach in the suburbs. What keeps us here? Hatred? I think not."

This was important feedback for the project. Yet I am reminded of the research of Kailin (1994), who maintains that many whites teach in the inner city by default. If more Branchard teachers had attended, some of these concerns could have been discussed before the peer performance. The students of color in the project did in fact perceive a greater amount of teacher-to-student racism than student-to-student racism. When expressing their experiences on stage during the "student expressions" act, these teacher-to-student experiences were prominent.

In discussions concerning the evaluations, students took on leadership roles to adjust the curriculum so that, before the performance, they would explain that not all teachers are racist but some are and these are the experiences that students have had with those racist teachers. In addition, students would mention that they experienced more racism from adults than from fellow students.

Teachers outside of the study site had more supportive comments about the curriculum. For instance, the middle school teachers were given the evaluation forms, and eight of approximately fifteen completed the survey. Similar to the "showing/work-in-progress performance" evaluations, the teachers felt this performance was a great means to "open people's eyes." All of the teachers supported this type of curriculum wholeheartedly. One possible reason why the suburban middle schools teachers were supportive is that I had worked as a multicultural education consultant, providing workshops for them for three years.

In the Middle School Arts Project, teachers also supported multicultural arts curricula. Their surveys consisted of twelve questions that dealt with their evaluation of the program, overall concerns in this area, and perceptions of multicultural arts education. For the most part, the teachers felt program objectives had been met, that racism did exist in the school system, and that the arts had a very unique advantage in teaching multicultural curriculum. Most agreed they would try more creative strategies in the classroom, but felt they needed additional education in both multicultural education and the arts. Each teacher felt these workshops would be welcomed throughout the school system, and that other teachers would be receptive to incorporating various styles of teaching and learning in their classrooms. In addition, these teachers felt that the administration would be supportive of infusing multicultural education into the school system's basic curriculum.

Yet it is interesting to note that many of the secondary teachers possessed opposite attitudes. Much of this can be attributed to the negative media exposure that Branchard High School received when one of the teachers made racist comments about the students. Many teachers felt they all were being accused of being racist. Doing the study project tended to inflame these attitudes.

This support study helped develop clarification on the role of the arts within multicultural education and the teacher and student interest level, which assisted the current study. In sharing these survey results with the high school participants, their leadership skills were once again sparked as this information motivated the students to create strategies and plan to reach out and perform for the younger students.

SUMMARY

This chapter has documented students' perceptions that racism exists in school and that it negatively affects their learning and behavioral development. In addition, they felt empowered through multicultural arts curricula to address issues of racism in school. Despite this empowerment they realized the difficulty of reaching others, especially adults. This is why the question was posed at the beginning of this chapter, "Who is willing to listen?"

The audience evaluations supported the above findings, in that the audience agreed that racism affects student learning and development, and that the arts within multicultural education curricula is a powerful tool to address such issues. These evaluations also helped underscore the ambivalence of teachers and administrators about supporting students in this type of endeavor. When the finger is not being pointed directly, such as for the elementary teachers and outside teachers, the comfort level of dealing with this issue appeared to be much more accepted.

The Student Race Relations Survey, done with two thousand students, confirmed the students' perceptions of racism in the Branchard school system. It also reinforced a finding from the project that students of color, especially African American students, perceive a greater amount of racism from teachers (adults) than from students.

It is important to understand that all children, whether victims, "white allies," or racists, are affected by racism. The next chapter begins with a classroom demonstration of a teacher making racist remarks. This beginning should remind us of the need to research teachers' racist attitudes and abilities to implement antiracist curricula.

Part III

THE TEACHER PROJECT—
AN ANTIRACIST PILOT STUDY
WITH TEACHERS

Chapter 6

Where Do We Go from Here?

EXAMINING THE ROLE OF TEACHERS

During a recent interview, Katina, a European American student, reflected on racist comments made by her seventh-grade social studies teacher. Part of her interview is as follows:

While on the subject of Africa one of the male students asked the teacher, "How did AIDS get started, because I've heard it started in Africa?" The teacher's response was that "AIDS was started by a gay black man who had sex with a monkey." The boys in the class began to make fun of gay people and people from Africa. The teacher allowed their laughter and negative comments. I didn't like the teacher putting down people with different backgrounds and race. African American students were often put down in class with the approval of this teacher. This teacher had taught at our school for twenty years and I had heard from other students that over the years he had humiliated many students. My mom came up to the school with me and requested a student/parent, teacher, and principal conference about the teacher's behavior. In the meeting, because the teacher refused to tell the truth, my mom stated that other students were willing to testify that he had said this. This put pressure on him to admit it. He said, "I may have been wrong about where AIDS came from, but I didn't mean anything by it." The principal said they had many complaints over the years, but he felt he had to protect the teachers in the system. At the end of the school year the teacher took an early retirement. I just feel bad about how many students must have been hurt by this teacher over that twenty-year period. (Interview, Donaldson, September 1995).

Katina is much like "Jessica" from the High School Project, in that she felt guilty and embarrassed by her teacher's actions. Her story gives an account of how an entire class can be affected by a teacher's biased attitudes. For example, the heritage of African American students was disparaged, "white allies" were discouraged, and other students' racist and homophobic views were reinforced. Although many cases are not as blatant as this one, whatever the degree of racism, teachers often state that they "don't mean any harm"; coupled with administrators who feel it is their duty to cover up, the damage done to students is generally severe.

This chapter highlights the Teacher Project, an antiracist curriculum development and implementation pilot study, with a variety of teachers from a small suburban/rural Midwest school district and the same urban New England school district used in the High School Project. By selecting different regions of the United States, geographical comparisons could be made.

As mentioned in the previous chapter, many students perceive their teachers as more likely to possess and project racist attitudes than their fellow students. For the most part, this is because they feel teachers are frequently in direct contact with them and have the authority and power to overrule them. Ramon, a member of SARIS, said to me, "No one would listen to a student reporting a teacher's racist attitudes" (Interview, Donaldson, June 1993).

Many students of color feel their safety and security hang in the balance when schools and educators allow racist attitudes to exist. Although many teachers care for all of their students and are not racist, it is important that educators understand how students feel and what teaching options are available in order to better address this educational crisis (Donaldson, 1994).

Although no teacher is immune to having racist attitudes, it is of particular concern for white teachers teaching in a multiracial society. For the most part, teachers of color have acquired a Eurocentric education, yet it is seldom the other way around. King (1991) asserts that many white educators experience "dysconscious racism"; they have been conditioned to have a limited and distorted view of cultural diversity and issues of racism, preventing them from supporting an equitable antiracist education.

Some scholars view racism as a pathological social disease of whites that can never be ended by antiracist education (Brown, 1995). They suggest that racial minorities should build and maintain their own schools to ensure student pride and success. Children in Afrocentric schools frequently surpass the academic achievement of students in the public school system (Ruenzel, 1994). These schools are very valuable in modeling education that enhances the success of African American students, but it is unlikely that every minority student will have the opportunity to attend a cultural academic private school in the immediate future. What would society be like if we attempted to separate students totally by race and ethnicity? Haven't we been down that road before? For example, in 1954 a landmark decision was made in the *Brown v. Board of Education* case; the Supreme Court ruled that school segregation was inherently unequal. Many Americans, from both the Left and the Right, may argue that segregation is best for all, or that schools are already segregated by homogenous communities. Yet it does not seem practical with our rapidly changing demographics to seek cultural isolation during one's school years. Instead, as tax payers, all U.S. citizens must demand equity and excellence for their schools, as well as hold all involved, including school administrators and teachers, accountable for providing curriculum that reflects the actual diversity in our schools. By choosing "flight," the problem of racism in schools is not addressed.

Nieto (1994) advocates multicultural education schools in which teachers acknowledge the diverse qualities that all students bring to school and have high expectations of each student. Using these concepts, public schools must recruit and/or educate teachers about antiracist/multicultural education. Together, we must ponder these issues. We need to examine whether a reeducation process for teachers can change racist attitudes.

UNDERSTANDING THE REEDUCATION PROCESS FOR TEACHERS

We must ask ourselves, "How do I feel about race and racism?", "Do I ever think about it?", and "If students are experiencing racism, shouldn't I try to understand it?" Understanding that there are developmental stages of racial awareness can make it easier to go through the process of examining our own racial conditioning.

A number of scholars stress the importance of educators recognizing their own racial identity development in order to better serve students of various racial and cultural backgrounds (Helms, 1990; Cross, 1991; Carter & Goodwin, 1994; Lawrence and Tatum, 1995). Carter and Goodwin (1994) describe racial identity as the psychological orientation toward one's racial group.

Tatum (1995) combines racial identity models from Helms (1990) and Cross (1991) with her own identity research with pre- and in-service teachers. She shares stages of racial/ethnic identity development in the United States for people of color and whites, and uses this research to explore teacher attitudes in the classroom.

In Tatum's recent course-study (1995), antiracist education proved to be of great benefit for white teacher-participants. According to Tatum, teachers were impacted in the following ways: (1) they gained awareness of race and racism; (2) they altered their thinking about themselves as racial beings; and (3) they learned new ways of thinking that moved them to change some of their behaviors regarding race. Small studies (less than forty participants) such as these have been few and far between; because of this rarity, they are valuable to the quest of reducing racism in schools.

Both Sleeter (1992) and Tatum (1995) agree that research in the area of antiracist education for teachers has been limited. Sleeter's exploration of teacher/staff development and multicultural education sought to prepare teachers to work more effectively with culturally diverse students. This two-year study engaged thirty white female teachers in a series of antiracist/multicultural education workshops. Teachers were able to examine their own attitudes about race. The study had hoped to reach higher stages of development levels, such as "acceptance" (learning about cultural diversity) and "affirmation" (developing new teaching skills). After fourteen all-day sessions, teachers were still at the awareness level. Sleeter's study helped confirm the degree of reeducation necessary for in-service teachers.

According to Kailin (1994), in order to reduce racism in schools teacher participation is required. Yet teachers are reluctant to join in the process. "Donna," from the project, wanted teachers to know that students were not against them, but that they were against racism in their schools. She suggested that since teachers appeared afraid of the subject, that students go to the teachers to dialogue. Eventually, we hope that this will be possible, but having assessed the need of teachers to broaden their awareness first, I have designed a study that indirectly shares perceptions of students with teachers.

The Teacher Project is a follow-up to the High School Project, where the results indicated a significant need to change the racist attitudes and actions of teachers. By understanding the experiences of students, teachers may be encouraged to reexamine their own attitudes and styles of teaching.

THE TEACHER PROJECT

The Antiracist Curriculum Development and Implementation Pilot Study was administered between March 1995 and June 1995. Through the participation of 119 school teachers (65% European American, 14% African American, 7% Native American, 6% biracial American, 2% Asian American, 1% Latino American; 74% female, 26% male; 42% Iowa teachers, 58% Massachusetts teachers) baselines of how teachers perceive racism in schools and ways of combatting it through antiracist curricula were established. Five instruments of study were developed and administered to participating teachers during the pilot study. These included: (1) teacher preliminary and post race relation surveys, (2) antiracist pilot curriculum handbooks for teachers, (3) antiracist pilot computer software and videos, (4) teacher midpoint surveys, and (5) teacher multimedia surveys. In addition, the pilot study includes pre and post student evaluations of teacher-participants, and teacher-participant focus group evaluation interviews.

The pilot study's preliminary survey produced empirical results that reflect a respectable degree of reliability ($r = 0.78$). The responses from this survey indicate the need to pursue further research; for example, 84.5 percent of the participating teachers agree that racism exists in schools. Furthermore, 88.2 percent agree that antiracist curricula is one key to addressing racism in schools.

Attempting to address the varied learning styles of participants, the antiracist pilot curriculum handbook and multimedia instruments emphasized creative and computer technology approaches to examining teachers' abilities to instruct in antiracist/multicultural education. The handbook consists of four chapters: (1) "Examining Attitudes about Racism"; (2) "Review of Racism in U.S. Schools"; (3) "Racism from the Student Perspective"; and (4) "Antiracist Lessons for K–12 Schools." Although I designed the overall handbook, input from the High School Project students was given. In addition to the curriculum instruments being prereviewed by students (high school and college level) and antiracist curriculum experts, the pilot study teacher-participants also provided feedback. Some of these teachers' responses included: "The handbook made me think about what material I was choosing and using, as well as my own ideas about racism"; and "I am a multimedia specialist and never before have I seen antiracist software [the *Africa to America* lesson from the High School Project was put in the teacher handbook and was also designed as software]. This makes me very excited."

Through the pilot study both qualitative and quantitative data were collected and analyzed to address the following questions:

1. Is there a change in teacher attitudes toward racism during the study? Or after exposure to the curriculum?

2. Is there a difference in attitudes toward racism by geographical area?

3. What problems do teachers have implementing antiracist curricula?

4. Can general classroom teachers successfully administer "student point of view," arts-based curriculum in the classroom?

5. Can multimedia heighten teacher antiracist education?

The teacher-participants were divided into five study groups: (1) those who completed the preliminary and post surveys only; (2) those who completed the preliminary, midpoint, and post surveys and received the curriculum study handbook without antiracist workshops; (3) those who completed the preliminary, midpoint, and post surveys, and received the curriculum study handbook with antiracist workshops; (4) those who completed the preliminary, midpoint, and post surveys, and received the curriculum study handbook with antiracist multimedia instruments; and (5) those who completed all of the above.

This manner of investigation enabled the development of a baseline for how teachers feel about racism in schools and whether they are able to implement codesigned student antiracist curriculum when guides, multimedia, and education workshops are made available to them. This method explored and compared to what degree teachers demonstrate change or ideological movement when exposed to different levels of antiracist materials. In addition, the study components assisted in the examination of the role of the arts and multimedia technology within antiracist/multicultural education.

The curriculum handbook, workshops, and multimedia consisted of creative ideas to explore issues of racism in schools. One goal of this emphasis was to answer the call of students, such as those in SARIS, who had the desire to share with teachers ways in which they felt they wanted to be taught (for instance, with encouragement and with multicultural materials and teaching strategies). SARIS donated their project play and theme song to this teacher study with the hope that teachers will become more sensitive to their plight and implement their codesigned materials in the classroom. The evaluation of this pilot study focuses on the enhancement of skills to address issues of racism in schools and to determine whether the curriculum model used is a viable tool for teachers implementing antiracist curriculum in their classrooms. The data collected provide evidence of teacher growth in racism awareness.

The teacher race awareness survey yielded some very interesting results. Project analyst Anthony Stevens reports the following: (1) All of the southern-born teachers agreed that racism is defined as a system of privilege and penalty based on one's race, as did nearly all of the Midwest-born teachers. Only 54.2 percent of the northern-born teachers agreed with this question. It would seem that exposure to blatant racism may have contributed to a better understanding of what racism is for these teachers. (2) Only 49.5 percent of the teachers surveyed agreed that racism is largely manifested in schools through biased curriculum and instruction. This is where the heart of the matter lies, and we clearly have work to do in this area. (3) It was found that teachers who grew up in families that promoted racist beliefs (Q27) reported having made unintentional racist/stereotypical comments in the classroom (Q25) more than those who did not grow up in racist households. (4) Older teachers agreed more strongly with the statement that racism exists within most U.S. schools (Q4) than younger teachers did. Additional empirical results from the preliminary survey, including reliability, regressions, t-tests, and path analysis are included in appendix D.

Field notes from the Teacher Project workshops help give a more in-depth view of the teachers' abilities to address racist attitudes within themselves, their students, racism in the curriculum, and the total school environment. The workshops were presented in a three-part series: (1) review of research and student points of views (with SARIS video); (2) self-awareness, antiracist exercises; and (3) antiracist curriculum implementation. Each workshop was approximately three hours in length. Teachers used the antiracist handbooks (codesigned by the High School Project students) during the workshops and responded on the reflection page after each chapter. In addition to participating in the three workshops, teachers who consented to actual classroom implementation with student surveys and teacher focus group interviews are currently receiving antiracist education classroom visits by project specialists. This section focuses on the three workshops only.

Six schools participated in the pilot study (Midwest: one high school, one middle school, two elementary schools; New England: one high school and one middle/elementary school). Teacher participation was encouraged through faculty meeting presentations. With the exception of one New England elementary school, where the principal made it part of their school improvement plan and required all the teachers to participate, all other teachers volunteered for the study.

Each school generated a different time schedule, some spanning beyond the pilot study timeframe of March 1995–June 1995. Because of this extension, all of the preliminary school sites have been moved into the larger study that encompasses four regions of the United States. Both administrators and teachers had concerns about their time commitment to the Teacher Project. In response to administrator release time anxieties, the workshops were scheduled not to exceed ten release time hours. These varied time approaches are discussed to demonstrate the flexibility necessary when doing an antiracist teacher project. By sharing highlights of the Teacher Project workshops, I hope that other schools will become interested in providing antiracist education for teachers.

WORKSHOP ONE

During the first workshop Midwest teachers, from all grade levels, listened attentively and remarked that they were very pleased to receive up-to-date research on racism in U.S. schools. They appeared annoyed by the racist treatment students received from teachers in the High School Project. On the other hand, at the high school site in New England, which is not the high school used in the High School Project, some teachers felt the students were exaggerating their experiences. I read this as a form of denial since the teacher-participants were exposed to numerous student reports with similar racist experiences by teachers, making it hard to believe that the students were embellishing.

The elementary school site in New England, as mentioned previously, required all teachers to participate. Some highlights of the field notes are as follows. During the second workshop, teachers enjoyed the added assistance in understanding the antiracist curriculum handbook, especially the antiracist conditioning exercises. Teachers remarked that they felt closer sharing their personal stories of racist experiences. The teachers of color remarked that they learned that whites experience racial prejudice as well. The African American and Latina teachers could share racist encounters on a daily basis. Their stories made clear that the frequency of racist acts toward people of color is greater than those of white teachers, who typically reported one or two racist experiences. The principal stated that she had always wanted the teachers to work together as a family, but until then, it had not happened. This workshop helped raise the awareness level of the teachers and lift the "taboo" of discussing issues of racism in schools.

Independent Control Group

The independent control group that was asked to cooperatively work through the handbook without the workshop said they did not get far with the exercises; although two of the teachers led the group in staying on task, not much was accomplished. This experience emphasizes the advantages of providing educational workshops with new curriculum.

WORKSHOP TWO

The second workshop for Midwest teachers also entailed self-awareness activities from the pilot handbook. Teachers examined the roots of racism in the United States, the melting pot theory, white privilege, and what being an "American" entails. In addition, they designed an imaginary racist society and compared it to past and present racial discrimination in the United States. The teachers reviewed Tatum's racial identity stages of development model (1995). They followed that with participation in some dismantling racism exercises. These exercises included times in which they witnessed racism, stood up against racism, and did nothing. The teachers concluded this exercise with envisioning a world without racism and practical goal setting (Fry, 1990).

The Midwest teachers were open and willing to share their experiences. They had concerns about how to respond to students who get upset when teachers mistake them for other students of color. It was recommended that they work on not confusing the students. Another teacher wanted to know how to handle black males when they appear to be arguing or getting ready to fight. This was an important question to address because so often African American males are perceived by white teachers as physically threatening. His question came after sharing the story of a teacher who thought a black student was being too sensitive when he was asked to stop playing rough with a "smaller white kid" [the teacher's expression], and the black student responded, "Why do you have to call my name first when he started it?" We talked about an African American tradition known as the "dozens," or in more recent times called "slamming" or "snapping." Slamming happens when two or more persons engage in a match of insults. It is generally a match of wits rather than physical confrontation. During this discussion I mentioned that I knew of an English teacher who had used "slamming" as a teaching tool to demonstrate "ebonics," black English, in which African words, phonetics, and traditions are maintained in African American culture despite the severing of direct ties to the African continent through forced immigration and slavery. The one African American male teacher in the group remarked that he would like to have that lesson, and he offered a solution when "slamming" appears to get out of hand. He said, "I've encountered this only on one or two occasions. My initial response was to get the students to discuss what they were doing and why they were doing it, and what kind of understanding were they taking from it. I then asked the question, 'How do you suppose other students would view this as they see you interacting in this way? You and your friends are able to communicate and get along quite well, but what if a white student walks up and says the same thing to you, how are you going to respond?' They replied, 'I'd punch them in mouth.'" The teacher concluded by saying, "That's part of the danger, you need to understand the environment in which you're in if you're going to engage in that type of interaction here. Someone else is going to think that it is okay for them to do the same, and if they have not established the same close bond with you, you may not accept it. Some of them said they could kind of see what I was saying." The point is that this teacher responded in a proactive manner rather than sending the students to the office to be disciplined.

The teachers greatly appreciated the workshop because options were shared on how to respond to racial and cultural situations. In addition, they felt it had given them a better understanding of how so many Americans are conditioned to be racist. They realized that there are exercises available to work on self-awareness and on changes within the classroom setting. Several of the teachers have begun the implementation process with a group of students of color who requested that a support group be formed to address issues of racism at their school. The teachers have called to report that the antiracist education they received has helped tremendously with facilitating the student group.

WORKSHOP THREE

The third workshop on integrating antiracist education into basic subject areas, such as social studies, took place at the start of a new school year. There was a high turnover of teachers at the elementary New England site due to the district's teacher contract dilemma. It took the group quite a while to get settled down; many came in late. There were at least ten new teachers and teacher assistants present. A few teachers were taking notes, but most appeared disengaged and tired.

Energy picked up during the "From Africa to America" dance activity, but some teachers still looked at each other as if to question why they were doing the activity, or seemed unwilling or embarrassed to fully participate in the dance. About one-third of the group felt they had learned something. About one-third indicated that they would try a lesson like this one in their classrooms. One new (white male) teacher said that he could not teach a lesson such as this because it went against his Christian beliefs to dance in praise of the sun, rain, and earth. Although I shared with him that this was a cultural lesson to understand the roots of racism in America, and that most of his students were of African American descent and could fully appreciate learning about their history, he was not moved. Another new (white female) teacher responded by saying that "this lesson might be hard for kids who come from a racist family because it would be confusing; they would be told that their family is wrong." In response to her comment, one of the teachers who had attended prior workshops said, "We can't control parents' ideas, but in the classroom we are a family and can discuss prejudice."

Four teachers from this elementary school have signed up for the classroom antiracist implementation component of the study. Through this study-component teachers will integrate antiracist views into basic curricula, teach antiracist units, and facilitate special projects and support groups for students. These forthcoming results should prove helpful because the study circles back to the students' point of view; students will evaluate the antiracist lessons delivered by their classroom teachers. In addition, teachers will share their experiences of teaching antiracist education. The other sites in the Teacher Project have not yet completed the workshops. In spite of this ongoing process, New England teacher-participants did the post surveys in June 1995, because of the turnover anticipated for the fall of 1995. This early post test enables us to analyze teacher growth in a series of longitudinal increments. Overall, the Teacher Project has helped create a series of baselines for further development and models for teachers to implement.

TEACHER PROJECT SUMMARY

Working with teachers in this project has restored my faith that there are teachers who care deeply about the well-being of all of their students and are willing to reeducate themselves regarding the issue of racism that plagues so many students. I realize that I have not sugarcoated the gap between many students of color and white teachers because it is necessary for teachers to recognize some of the "real" problems as identified by the students and antiracist education research. Yet all teachers need to know that they are appreciated in the struggle of creating racism-free school environments. Teachers are an integral part of the wheel that makes the world go around. Without teachers our nation would not be as well educated or as prosperous.

To date, the study has revealed some significant findings. Many teachers acknowledge the existence of racism in schools and that antiracist education is one key alternative to addressing this problem. Although many teachers denied that racism is manifested in biased curriculum and instruction, those who participated in the curriculum components tended to change their view. The study reinforced other antiracist education research presented in this chapter with regard to the need for ongoing reeducation.

These and other findings from the pilot study were encouraging as I attempt to document research and to address racist attitudes in schools. The methods used for the pilot study are being repeated in the larger study. The goal of the larger study is to broaden teacher participation, thereby developing greater baseline figures. The official study results will be available in August 1996. The study will include approximately three hundred teachers from several regions of the United States, including the South, West, Midwest, and Northeast. The study highlights urban, suburban, and rural teacher responses. The goal of the wide coverage is to discover and compare outlooks and needs of U.S. teachers in a variety of geographical settings with diverse population demographics.

RECOMMENDATIONS FOR THE TOTAL SCHOOL ENVIRONMENT

Racism in schools and the efforts to reduce it should concern the total school environment. This environment includes all school personnel, students, parents, local communities, and the federal government. Since students are the most affected by racism in schools, it is recommended that they have a major role in getting others to recognize the seriousness of the situation. As students dialogue and perform antiracist scripts for different classrooms to heighten the consciousness of this social and school dilemma, adults need to get on board. Students cannot successfully attack racism without adult support or allies within the school system.

For the most part, there is no national consensus on the importance of multicultural curriculum offered in schools, but teachers and administrators can help in numerous ways. They can follow up on student concerns in the classroom and the general school setting by insisting that schools provide multicultural curricula and educational courses for teachers. Racism and prejudice units can be designed at all grade levels. Student peer teaching in curriculum development should be encouraged. Students, such as the participants in the High School Project or in the Middle School Multicultural Club who were taught about racism, can make a series of visits to different classrooms, working with teachers and students to raise awareness about curriculum that addresses the issue of racism. In addition, a professional videotape of student performances, including their process and discussions, can be produced and made available to participating schools, as well as antiracist study instruments.

School policy can be enhanced to directly address racism in schools. Administrators can honor these policies by publicly discussing them with staff and students and visibly placing them where all can see, as in the case of the Oregon middle school mentioned earlier. Administrators must be at the forefront of the movement, actively supporting antibias efforts. Colleges of education can bolster recruitment strategies for students of color and provide viable multicultural education programs. In turn, K–12 administrators can hire teachers of diverse backgrounds whenever possible to add to multicultural efforts in their schools. Administrators can also seek alternatives such as cooperative learning, instead of tracking and ability grouping, as well as diversity-sensitive standardized testing. They can schedule antiracist/multicultural teacher education workshops and give incentives for teachers who receive multicultural education certification. Antiracist/multicultural support groups can be formed for the total school community.

Schools need to intentionally integrate antiracist projects within their programs. Educators must write proposals and prepare school budgets with these programs in mind. This funding can be used to infuse both the arts and multicultural education into classrooms because these two components of education are of great interest to students.

It is important to view racism in schools as a national crisis that will directly or indirectly affect all students as well as society as a whole. With this in mind, perhaps we can recognize the urgency of addressing it at both the national and local levels.

The consideration of combining antiracist/multicultural arts education needs to take place. Antiracist/multicultural education advocates need to band together to put pressure on the federal government and local communities to enforce multicultural education reform for public education. In addition, art educators need to join in this struggle and promote the arts within multicultural education as a necessary component of education for modern classrooms.

SUGGESTIONS FOR FUTURE RESEARCH

In the study conducted by Murray and Clark (1990), both researchers agreed that little research had been done on what students perceive as racism in school. Because it is important for educators to recognize the existence of racism and its adverse effects on schoolchildren, we must continue to conduct studies in this area. A strong research base on racism in schools increases the likelihood that educators will recognize racism in their own schools and realize the benefits of eradicating it for all involved.

The High School Project sought to examine the perceptions of a small high school sample population. Yet race relations need to be further explored among K–12 students, as well as among school personnel, preservice educators, curriculum planners, curriculum publishers, parents, and the community. For instance, studies focusing on conditions in schools that help improve interethnic relations between teachers and students of different backgrounds might be helpful. In addition, studies that explore parent and community perceptions of racism may assist in encouraging them to support antiracist education. Since many teachers feel multicultural curricular materials are inaccessible in schools, studies can be conducted to determine the interest of publishers and curriculum planners to produce antiracist/multicultural textbooks and curricula for classroom use. In regard to preservice educators, many education/certification programs such as the education programs at Iowa State University and the University of Massachusetts require students to take multicultural education courses. Follow-up on how these students utilize this training in the actual classroom would be beneficial for the overall reeducation process for teachers and for the refinement of the courses.

Since studies reveal that students of color perceive racism more from teachers than from their peers, a more in-depth study should be done. Both student and teacher attitudes should be researched to address why many white teachers fear addressing issues of racism. Such research could be helpful in designing professional development programs, such as the Teacher Project. It is also necessary to further explore the connection among racism, student underachievement, and the high dropout rates of students of color.

Further research must also be developed to study the arts within multicultural education in order to demonstrate the significance of this component as part of the basic curriculum. Both the arts and multicultural education have been seen as additives to the curriculum; yet many students feel otherwise. Finally, more research needs to be done on peer education and student curriculum development.

CONCLUSION

In the text I have explored how racism is manifested in schools, how racism affects student learning, and how antiracist/multicultural arts curricula can address racism in schools. I have focused on racism in schools from the students' point of view and used their solutions to develop student and teacher antiracist education models.

This work can benefit the entire school environment. The more we understand the perceptions and needs of our students, the more we can offer excellence in the educational setting. Creating a better education system requires that schools be studied within the social context of U.S. society and that our country rids itself of racism. As students are able to think for themselves and establish antiracist attitudes and behaviors, these values can be incorporated in their everyday living. When children shine they radiate their energy to others. They provide needed leadership because the world today needs role models of all ages. The following SARIS theme song demonstrates such leadership.

> Let's stop racism in our schools
> Too many of us are hurt you see
> By this country's bigotry
> What we need is unity
> We all have the right
> To be treated with respect
> But until we see the light
> That something we'll never get
> All of our ancestors have given
> Much to this land

Why can't we appreciate this
and try to understand
Hand in hand we'll make a better earth
Let racism die
So that love can give birth
To see the beauty of you and me
In this land of diversity
Rid the violence and the pain
Can we sing that once again
Let's stop racism in our school
Look it right in the face
Say goodbye forever
Because here it has no place
If all races can unite
Talk it out without a fight
It will help us see the light
Then everything can be alright

SARIS 1993

Appendix A

High School Project

A.1.   Student Race Relations Survey

For each statement, check whether you strongly agree (SA), agree (A), are not sure (NS), disagree (D), or strongly disagree (SD).

	SA	A	NS	D	SD
In my school, all students are treated the same regardless of how they speak, dress, or act.	—	—	—	—	—
Teachers treat students differently because of race.	—	—	—	—	—
My counselor treats students differently because of race.	—	—	—	—	—
My principal or assistant principal treats students differently because of race.	—	—	—	—	—
Students in my school treat other students differently because of race.	—	—	—	—	—
My racial group is treated the same as any other.	—	—	—	—	—
I have been personally hurt because of racism in my school.	—	—	—	—	—

	SA	A	NS	D	SD

I have not been personally hurt because of racism in my school, but I have seen others hurt. — — — — —

In my school, success depends on a person's race. — — — — —

The teachers and principals in my school have helped to create good relations among students of different racial groups. — — — — —

The teachers and principals in my school have helped to create good relations among students of different racial groups. — — — — —

Discipline in my school is carried out fairly without regard to race. — — — — —

There is no racism in my school. — — — — —

How many times have you been suspended from school?

     0   1   2   3   4 or more

At what level were you first suspended?

     Elementary   Middle   High School

At what level were you last suspended?

     Elementary   Middle   High School

How many times have you been suspended internally?

     0   1   2   3   4 or more

At what level were you first suspended?

     Elementary   Middle   High School

At what level were you last suspended?

     Elementary   Middle   High School

On the back, write your definition of racism.

If racism is a problem, how would you solve it?

A.2. *Interview Questions*

1. What are some of your perceptions and experiences of racism in schools?

2. Does racism affect student learning and behavior? If so, give specific examples.

3. What does it mean to you to take on a leadership role in the development of an antiracist/multicultural education curriculum?

4. Do you think students should have more input in the development of curriculum? Explain.

5. How did you feel about developing a racism awareness production and performing it for teachers, administrators, fellow students, and the community?

6. Do you enjoy learning basic subjects using the arts and media?

7. Name some of the ways you learn best.

8. Would you be more motivated to want to finish school if these various ways of learning were incorporated into the school curriculum?

9. Can the arts in multicultural education address the varied learning styles of students?

10. Please explain why students may like or dislike using the arts to learn basic education (multicultural education)?

11. How do you anticipate this curriculum helping to reduce racism in the schools?

12. Would you recommend this curriculum model to other schools? Why or why not?

13. How has this curriculum of multicultural education, the arts, and media empowered you to address racism?

14. As a participant in the study project, do you have any suggestions for improvement? Is there anything you would have done differently from the project director? Explain.

A.3.   "Let's Stop Racism in Our Schools" Script

"Let's Stop Racism in Our Schools" is a forty-five-minute production showing how racism affects student learning and interest. The production begins with a student protest rally to stop racism in the schools. It then traces the roots of racism in the United States, and investigates in part institutionalized racism as it affects U.S. school systems. The finale expresses the need for Americans to learn of one another's contributions to the United States, in order to appreciate and excel even further as a diverse nation.

The purpose of this production is to give students the opportunity to voice their concerns about racism in the schools and in their nation. It further allows the students to take leadership roles in developing an antiracism awareness model to be used by schools throughout the country.

OPENING

Music Playing: Harold Melvin and The Bluenotes, "Wake Up Everybody."
Students enter from stage right and stage left with picket signs that read Stop Racism.

Scene 1

Protest March

>   *Entire Cast:* Stop Racism in America! Stop Racism in Our Schools!

(Cast repeats these phrases until everyone is in position.)
(Step dance begins [to demonstrate strength and determination, and to clear posters from the stage].)

>   *Cast:*   We march for you to see
>   That racism hurts you and me
>   Step dance—Where is it from?
>   Africa—where you hear the drum
>   Racism is here and there
>   South Africa and everywhere
>   In South Africa step dance is a boot dance
>   That shows the oppression
>   Let's pass our protest signs down now
>   And get on with our racism lesson . . .
>   It's in our schools and in our towns
>   Racism is all around

(Expressions begin: one at a time selected students share their encounters with racism)

Student 1: During my English class someone blurted out the word *nigger*. Being the only African American in the class, everyone turned and looked at me. I thought the word *nigger* meant ignorant person. That certainly doesn't apply to me. I feel they should have looked at the ignorant person that made the statement. Stop Racism in Our Schools!

Student 2: As I entered my new class the teacher automatically stopped me and asked if I was in the right class. As I looked around and saw that I was the only Spanish person there, it dawned on me that she thought I should have not been placed in an advanced class. Once I showed her my class schedule, she then asks if I'm sure I want to be there. I answered yes, and then she warned me not to get out of line while in her class. A few weeks later she came up to me and said, "You're not what I expected you to be. You're a good kid." Why is it that I was prejudged by my race to begin with? Stop Racism in Our Schools!

Student 3: Because of my accent I was placed in special education classes for slower children. I wasn't even tested, and was kept there for half of the year before I was placed into regular classes. How could this have happened? Stop Racism in Our Schools!

Student 4: If you're a person of color and wearing baggy clothes and hoodies, and you're in the halls, teachers are apt to ask you for a pass. If you're white and dressed in regular clothes, teachers oftentimes will not ask if you have a pass. Why is that? Stop Racism in Our Schools!

Student 5: I have friends of all races in school. Oftentimes we hear from our own peers things like, "Why don't you stick with your own kind?" Why can't we all be friends and respect one another? We are all in school for the same reason, to learn. Why can't we learn that racism hurts all of us? Stop Racism in Our Schools!

Narrator: Racism is the false belief that one race of people is superior to or better than another race. Racism is a system of privilege and penalty based on one's race. Racism is on the rise in schools throughout our nation. Statistics show that students of color are more often the targets of racism than white students. Students of color experience racial slurs, discrimination, and omission of their cultural contribution in schoolbooks and curriculum. Racism is a negative factor that makes potentially great students disinterested in school. America needs all its youth educated in order to remain one of the world's leading nations in productivity. Stop Racism in America!

Student 6: How did racism get started in America anyway?

Student 7: It goes as far back as Christopher Columbus when he landed on the island of San Salvador.

(Cast take positions for scene 2)

Scene 2

Sailor: Land ho, Columbus!

Columbus: Bless the land for Queen Isabella!

(Columbus and the sailor hop off the ship onto the island. The Tainos and the Arawak people welcome them. The chief claps his hands so the people can bring gifts to Columbus. Columbus then turns to the sailor to write a letter to Queen Isabella of Spain.)

Columbus: Dear Queen Isabella, I have been to this great land of gold and spices. The natives are friendly and have taught us many things about the land. These gentle savages can be easily subdued and made into slaves so that we can bring the riches of this land to Spain. [*Columbus then tells the sailor . . .*] Take the chief and his people captive. Send the young ones to get gold; cut their hands off if they disobey; and put the others on the ship to bring back to Spain.

Narrator: Many of the Tainos and Arawak people of the island were killed. Those who were brought back to Spain died also. It was determined that the people would not make good slaves, so Europe had to look elsewhere for help to strip the new lands of its riches. It turned to Africa.

Narrator 2: Europe had been trading for many centuries with Africa. People from Europe and other parts of the world came to Africa to study history, law, and medicine. Once the New World became Europe's major source of gold, the ancient African trade routes were no longer profitable. European traders coaxed many kings of Africa to let Africans go to help Europeans in the New World. It was then greedy merchants realized the hard labor of the Africans was very profitable. The merchants began to pay raiders to go into African villages and kidnap the African people. They forced the African people into chains and onto ships and sold them in the New World as slaves. Over 50 million Africans were stolen from Africa and forced to come to the Americas.

Narrator 3: At this same time the Native American Indians were being wiped out and off the lands to make room for the Europeans. Many Europeans who were profiting from the enslavement of Africans and the killing of Indians were troubled because their religious beliefs, moral convictions, and value of human life conflicted with their greed. This is one reason racism developed.

Merchant: (*To the auctioneer*) In order to justify selling these Africans, call them the lowest names you can think of. Make them appear like they are not human, like we do them Indians. Make our kind feel like anyone who does not look like them are heathens and an inferior race.

Auctioneer: Yes sir, Mr. Merchant. Fine niggers here. Fine niggers here for sale! These wretched jungle bunny-coons are strong and will build up your plantations, making you and your descendants rich for life! How 'bout this one? (*Pulls an African woman out —she starts to weep*) She'd make a fine nanny, maid, or mistress, and this one? (*Pulls an African male out—he is resistant*) Yeah . . . they are like animals . . . they ain't got no thoughts or feelings.

Narrator 4: Though slavery was abolished, racism remained alive and well. There was segregation to keep people of color down—the Jim Crow laws for blacks, reservations for Indians, and segregated towns for the Asians, who were used as cheap labor after slavery.

Narrator 5: As America grew the dominant society stayed intact and created the melting pot for newcomers. Even European immigrants had to give up their ethnic cultures, names, and native languages to blend in and be accepted.

Narrator 6: People of color such as Latinos could not blend in because their culture was different and they experienced exclusion and racism like the African, Native American, and Asian groups. Racism shut out (*Cast becomes the mainstream and forms a circle—with the exception of the narrators who have stepped forward; the narrators become outcast*) the culture of the Native people and other people (*Narrators are trying to become part of the mainstream circle, but the circle will not allow them*) who contributed their labor. (*One at a time the group will join the narrators center stage in a picture pose, making closing remarks*)

Cast: (*Joining in with the narrator*) . . . Blood, sweat, and tears!

Student 1: (*Continues*) . . . Ideas, inventions, artistry . . .

Student 2: In many history and literature books at school you cannot learn about the contributions or experiences of people of color.

Student 3: Though we are diverse, ways of learning are limited in school.

Student 4: As students we often become disinterested when classes don't relate to our experiences.

Student 5: Or when teachers dole out punishment unfairly, not recognizing we are bored.

Student 6: Of course, this leaves room for us to pick on one another, reflecting a new racism. *Everybody hates everyone who is not like them.*

Student 7: Racism has hurt everyone.

Student 1: It's denied America its true beauty.

Student 2: It's made whites feel guilty and real confused.

Student 3: It has violently oppressed and denied access to people of color.

Student 4: If you think you're better than someone else, you generally look down on them even when you don't realize it.

Student 5: If you think you are less than someone else, you generally give up before you ever get started.

Student 6: We are young, diverse, and the leaders of tomorrow.

Student 7: We are saying what we feel in hopes that people will listen and things will change, that students everywhere will work hard at their studies and their understanding of others because that's the only way we are going to survive in the twenty-first century.

Student 1: We need our teachers, administrators, parents, and communities to love and be proud of all of us.

Student 2: . . . Treat us fairly, mentor us, and educate us well in all areas, especially our nation's history.

Student 3: If we know our past we can prepare better for the future.

Student 4: Let's stop racism in our schools! (*Cast sings: "Let's Stop Racism in Our Schools"*)

The End   [OPEN DISCUSSION]

A.4.   *Audience Evaluation Survey*

AUDIENCE EVALUATION SURVEY

Please circle gender: male   female

What is your ethnic background?

Please circle current status:
1. student   [grade _____]
2. teacher   [grade _____]
3. school administrator
4. parent
5. community agency representative
6. other (please describe affiliation)

1. Do you believe this production/curriculum can be helpful in reducing racism in U.S. schools? Why or why not?

2. Would you actively support it? If yes, how? If no, please explain.

3. In your opinion, does racism affect students' learning? Please explain.

4. Would you like to see this type of multicultural arts curriculum developed for regular classroom use? Why or why not?

5.   What is your opinion of students assisting in the development of multicultural curricula?

Please write any additional comments on the back.

AUDIENCE EVALUATIONS SURVEY RESULTS

"Let's Stop Racism In Our Schools"

April 13, 1993
Branchard High School/Showing Performance
Total number of respondents: 17

Demographic breakdown:

Ethnic Background	Gender	Status
5 white female	13 female	1 teacher
2 Hispanic	1 male	4 parent
1 Native American/Cherokee	3 unidentified	1 school administrator
1 African American/white		1 city representative
1 African American/Indian		2 community agency representative
6 unidentified		2 Healing Racism Institute
		2 school employee/ mediation program

Question 1: Do you believe this production/curriculum can be helpful in reducing racism in U.S. schools?
Yes - 17

Question 2: Would you actively support it?
Yes - 13   Unsure - 1   No response - 3

Question 3: In your opinion, does racism affect students' learning?
Response - 12   No response - 4
Sample responses: More teachers to give their opinions. Bring it out to the public. Students could exude more confidence in speaking. It

could describe more backgrounds. I think it looks great already. Integration of more ethnic groups.

Question 4: Would you like to see this type of multicultural arts curriculum developed for regular classroom use?
Response - 16   No response - 1
Sample responses: Positive experience that should be available to all students. Should be included in regular classrooms whenever possible. Excellent idea. Absolutely needed. Racism is very real and this type of multicultural curriculum is necessary if the human race is going to unite and work together.

Question 5: What is your opinion of students assisting in the development of multicultural curricula?
Response - 14   No response - 3
Sample responses: Multicultural education must be present in all subjects at school because of our diverse population. Where practical— fine. Long overdue. It's crucial in today's world.

April 16, 1993
Suburban Middle School Performance
Total number of respondents: 8 (all teachers)

Demographic breakdown:

Ethnic Background   Gender
8 European-American   6 female
                                                        2 male

Question 1: Do you believe this production/curriculum can be helpful in reducing racism in U.S. schools?
Yes - 6   Unsure - 1   No - 2 ("good start, but it won't
                                                   reduce racism alone")

Question 2: Would you actively support it?
Yes - 6   No - 1   No response - 2

Question 3: In your opinion, does racism affect students' learning?
Response - 8

Sample responses: How about more of a mix of all races? Q&A period would be better in smaller groups. Never give up, keep striving to make the program better. Act out one or two of the incidents with the students.

Question 4: Would you like to see this type of multicultural arts curriculum developed for regular classroom use?
Response - 8

Sample responses: The multicultural and multimedia combo is excellent, my students say they learn best that way. It should be started in kindergarten. It will cost more money than the school systems will/can afford. The kids need to see it and feel it.

Question 5: What is your opinion of students assisting in the development of multicultural curricula?
Response - 8

Sample responses: At all times in all subject areas, until the day this question will not matter. I support it 100 percent. It's the only way to break the insidious chain of racism. We need to be educated in all areas.

June 1, 1993
Branchard High School Performance
Total number of respondents: 47

Demographic breakdown:

Ethnic Background
12 white
1 Hispanic
3 biracial
10 African American
21 unidentified

Status
2 teachers (one black/visiting
    fourth-grade teacher, one white
45 students

Question 1: Do you believe this production/curriculum can be helpful in reducing racism in U.S. schools?
Yes - 28   No - 14   Unsure - 5   No response - 5

[Results for Questions 2–5 will appear by ethnic grouping]

Question 2: Would you actively support it?
African American: Yes - 9; No response - 1
European American: Yes - 11; No response - 1
Biracial: Yes - 2; No response - 1
Hispanic Student: Yes
Unidentified Students: Yes - 14; No - 8

Question 3: In your opinion, does racism affect students' learning?
African American: Yes - 9; No response - 1
European American: Yes - 10; Unsure - 1; No - 1
Biracial: Yes - 1; Unsure - 1; No response - 1
Hispanic Student: Yes
Unidentified Students: Yes - 16; No - 5; No response - 1

Question 4: Would you like to see this type of multicultural arts curriculum developed for regular classroom use?
African American: Yes - 8; No response - 2
European American: Yes - 10; Unsure - 1; No - 1
Biracial: Yes - 3
Hispanic Student: Yes ("We need to learn more about each other, if we know about each other we'll understand more.")
Unidentified students: Yes - 15; No - 6; No response - 1

Question 5: What is your opinion of students assisting in the development of multicultural curricula?
African American: Good - 7; No response - 3
European American: Good - 10; Unsure - 1; No - 1 ("It would start fights.")
Biracial: Responses - 2 ("They made me feel proud."); No response - 1
Hispanic Student: ("It's very good. We need more students involved.")
Unidentified Students: Yes - 9; No - 7; No response - 6

Appendix B

Middle School Arts Project Surveys

PRELIMINARY STUDENT SURVEY QUESTIONS

1. What have you learned so far about the Westward Movement?

2. From the list choose three ways you learn best in the classroom: (a) reading, (b) listening, (c) watching, (d) hands-on activities/the arts, (e) writing, (f) communicating/discussions, (g) researching, (h) classroom visits.

3. Do you like to learn working in groups, as a team, or by yourself?

4. How would you like it if your teacher used the arts, such as drama, dance, and music, to teach you about your subjects?

5. Would you like to study about different cultures that have helped make America what it is today?

6. Take a guess at what you think multicultural education is.

7. Many educators say that there is a lot of racism and violence in the schools today. Can you describe what racism is and why it might be going on in schools?

8. Take a guess on how multicultural education can help this problem.

PRELIMINARY STUDENT SURVEY RESULTS

Table 1. Question 1: What have you learned so far about the Westward Movement?

	Knowledgeable	Somewhat knowledgeable	No knowledge
School #1			
Class A	7	3	12
Class B	9	10	5
Subtotal	16	13	17
School #2			
Class A	0	0	16
Class B	0	1	14
Class C	6	4	4
Subtotal	6	5	34
School #3			
Class A	12	7	2
Class B	1	0	21
Class C	0	10	12
Class D	2	4	19
Subtotal	15	21	54
Grand Total	37	39	105

Table 2. Question 2: From the list choose three ways you learn best
in the classroom: (a) reading, (b) listening, (c) watching,
(d) hands-on activities/the arts, (e) writing, (f) communicat-
ing/discussions, (g) researching, (h) classroom visits. (Top
three choices listed only.)

	School #1	School #2	School #3	Total
A. Reading	66	20	8	94
B. Listening	42	35	15	82
C. Watching	25	31	21	77
D. Hands-on/arts	25	24	17	66
E. Writing	5	20	15	40

Table 2. Continued.

	School #1	School #2	School #3	Total
F. Discussions	14	21	35	70
G. Researching	7	5	26	38
H. Class visits	7	20	38	65

Table 3. Question 3: Do you like to learn working in groups, as a team, or by yourself?

	Groups	Individual	Both	No response
School #1				
Class A	20	2	0	0
Class B	19	2	5	0
Subtotal	39	4	5	0
School #2				
Class A	11	3	1	1
Class B	12	3	0	0
Class C	7	1	7	0
Subtotal	30	7	8	1
School #3				
Class A	13	9	0	0
Class B	20	1	0	0
Class C	17	9	0	0
Class D	9	8	5	0
Subtotal	59	27	5	0
Grand Total	128	38	18	1

Table 4. Question 4: How would you like it if your teacher used the arts, such as drama, dance, and music, to teach you about your subjects?

	Yes	Sometimes	No	Don't know
School #1				
Class A	20	0	3	5
Class B	16	5	1	0
Subtotal	36	5	4	5
School #2				
Class A	14	0	1	1
Class B	7	0	9	0
Class C	14	0	0	0
Subtotal	35	0	10	1
School #3				
Class A	16	0	6	0
Class B	9	4	7	1
Class C	15	0	10	0
Class D	9	3	9	1
Subtotal	49	7	32	2
Grand Total	120	12	46	8

Question 5. Would you like to study about different cultures that have helped make America what it is today?
183 yes (all students)

Table 5. Question 6: Take a guess at what you think multicultural education is.

	Very knowledge-able	Knowledge-able	Somewhat knowledge-able	No knowledge
School #1				
Class A	1	0	1	20
Class B	0	4	6	17
Subtotal	1	4	7	37

Table 5. Continued.

	Very knowledge-able	Knowledge-able	Somewhat knowledge-able	No knowledge
School #2				
Class A	1	8	2	5
Class B	1	8	2	4
Class C	8	2	2	2
Subtotal	10	18	6	11
School #3				
Class A	0	8	6	8
Class B	2	11	6	6
Class C	1	6	6	8
Class D	0	6	3	13
Subtotal	3	31	21	35
Grand Total	14	53	34	83

Table 6. Question 7: Many educators say that there is a lot of racism and violence in the schools today. Can you describe what racism is and why it might be going on in schools?

	Very knowledge-able	Knowledge-able	Somewhat knowledge-able	Don't know
School #1				
Class A	0	8	5	13
Class B	1	8	2	11
Subtotal	1	16	7	24
School #2				
Class A	0	7	4	5
Class B	0	4	3	6
Class C	0	9	6	1
Subtotal	0	20	13	12

Table 6. Continued.

	Very knowledge-able	Knowledge-able	Somewhat knowledge-able	Don't know
School #3				
Class A	2	7	7	6
Class B	0	12	10	4
Class C	1	10	7	1
Class D	1	9	0	2
Subtotal	4	38	33	13
Grand Total	5	74	53	49

Table 7. Question 8: Take a guess on how multicultural education can help this problem.

	Knowledgeable	Somewhat knowledgeable	Don't know
School #1			
Class A	1	3	18
Class B	3	2	21
Subtotal	4	5	39
School #2			
Class A	8	2	5
Class B	7	2	5
Class C	5	6	4
Subtotal	20	10	14
School #3			
Class A	11	6	5
Class B	7	2	9
Class C	6	8	14
Class D	3	1	18
Subtotal	27	17	46
Grand Total	51	32	99

STUDENT POST-SURVEY QUESTIONS

1. What is multicultural education?

2. What is racism?

3. Which multicultural workshop did you like best?

4. How have these workshops helped you overall?

5. Would you like to do these and other cultural arts workshops again?

6. Additional comments?

STUDENT POST-SURVEY RESULTS

Table 1. Question 1: What is multicultural education?

	Knowledgeable	Somewhat knowledgeable	Don't know
School #1			
Class A	12	4	10
Class B	14	2	4
Subtotal	26	6	14
School #2			
Class A	9	1	1
Class B	14	0	3
Class C	8	3	0
Subtotal	31	4	4
School #3			
Class A	8	4	9
Class B	17	3	4
Class C	9	2	12
Class D	17	0	3
Subtotal	51	9	28
Grand Total	108	19	46

Table 2. Question 2: What is racism?

	Knowledgeable	Somewhat knowledgeable	Don't know
School #1			
Class A	14	1	5
Class B	17	4	5
Subtotal	31	5	10
School #2			
Class A	7	4	0
Class B	12	1	4
Class C	9	2	0
Subtotal	28	7	4
School #3			
Class A	17	3	0
Class B	8	8	6
Class C	13	7	4
Class D	13	5	2
Subtotal	51	23	12
Grand Total	110	35	26

Table 3. Question 3: Which multicultural workshop did you like best?

	African American	Native American	Both
School #1			
Class A	22	2	3
Class B	13	4	2
Subtotal	35	6	5
School #2			
Class A	5	2	9
Class B	5	3	3
Class C	5	1	8
Subtotal	15	6	20

Table 3. Continued

	African American	Native American	Both
School #3			
Class A	9	3	9
Class B	5	3	16
Class C	9	4	10
Class D	4	0	16
Subtotal	27	10	51
Grand Total	77	22	76

Question 4. How have these workshops helped you overall? (For qualitative responses, see next page.)

Table 4. Question 5: Would you like to do these and other cultural arts workshops again?

	Yes	No
School #1		
Class A	20	1
Class B	25	0
Subtotal	45	1
School #2		
Class A	12	0
Class B	11	0
Class C	18	0
Subtotal	41	0
School #3		
Class A	21	1
Class B	20	1
Class C	20	1
Class D	24	0
Subtotal	85	3
Grand Total	171	4

STUDENT POST-SURVEY: QUESTION # 4 QUALITATIVE RESPONSES

(After each written response an ethnic gender code will follow.)
Code description: W-F = White Female; B-F = Black Female; H-F =
Hispanic Female; W-M = White Male; B-M = Black Male; H-M =
Hispanic Male

1.   Learned new things. W-F

2.   Understand the Indians. W-M

3.   I learned about my ancestors and I liked it. B-F

4.   I learned that all Native Americans don't do what they show on TV. B-F

5.   I learned how Americans were treated wrong because of their color. H-F

6.   It helped me learn history from long ago. B-M

7.   It helped a lot, because if I take a test about it I'll know a lot about it and now I know how those people felt. H-M

8.   It showed me how bad it was for Native Americans and African Americans to be pushed out of their land and houses. H-F

9.   I used to think all Native American cultures were alike. B-M

10.   It helped me to realize what black people did before they became slaves. B-F

11.   That only Indian women make that kind of yell. M-W

12.   They have helped me see stereotypes. W-F

13.   They taught me dances and about the Westward Movement. W-M

14.   It helped me to learn the real stuff. B-F

15.   I've learned about African Americans. H-M

16.   Helped me to learn how it was to live like they lived. B-F

17.   I learned about other peoples' cultures and about life. W-F

18.   Helped us learn about the different kinds of Americans. W-M

19. We learned about cultures we never heard of. W-M

20. How people were treated and how they overcame it. W-M

21. It helped me learn that it's very different than people think. W-M

22. It helped a lot because when people ask I can help them learn. B-F

23. I learned more from people than the book. B-M

24. I learned more about culture and stories, like the Turtle. W-F

25. Before I went to them I thought almost all Indians and Africans were mean and loved war. I was wrong!! Mulatto-F

26. The workshops helped me realize what Americans did to other people, but also how others helped. W-F

27. It helped me realize the years of pain and suffering different races went through. W-F

28. Helped me in my multicultural class. H-F

29. It taught me to teach my family it. B-F

30. They helped me because now people get along better with you. H-M

31. These workshops made me angry. How could they treat people this way? B-F

32. It helped me feel a little bit of what the people felt. W-M

33. How different cultures helped to contribute to make America a better place. W-M

34. Life in general. B-M

35. Helped me understand more. W-F

TEACHER POST-SURVEY QUESTIONS

1. Did I attain the workshop goals and objectives?
   (a) teaching about other perspectives/contributions regarding the Westward Movement; which are not always included in social studies textbooks

   (b) teaching about the lifestyles/story of other cultures
   (c) teaching about the roots of racism and violence in the United States
   (d) encouraging respect for self and others

 2. Did you feel using varied teaching strategies, such as the arts, was beneficial? In what way?

 3. Will you as a teacher try to utilize some of these strategies?

 4. What do you think about multicultural education?

 5. Do you feel you have resources at your school to teach multiculturally?

 6. Do you feel that racism and violence exist in your school system?

 7. Would you suggest that these types of multicultural education workshops be offered throughout the system? Why or why not?

 8. How receptive do you feel teachers will be to restructuring their classes to incorporate various styles of teaching and learning?

 9. Do you feel the school administration is supportive of multicultural education as basic education in the schools?

 10. What have you done as follow-up to these workshops?

 11. What is your multicultural education thus far?

 12. Additional comments?

TEACHER POST-SURVEY QUALITATIVE RESULTS

The teachers at school #1 answered these questions orally. Their overall attitude toward the program, especially the African American workshop, was positive. They did make recommendations for future workshops, that only well-skilled artist/educators, such as myself, administer the workshops. These teachers' multicultural education backgrounds were very limited; they did not see themselves as able to teach multicultural arts education in their classrooms.

The teachers at school #2 varied in answers because of their experiences and cultural backgrounds. One of the white teachers did not fill out the demographic information on the survey, which asked her age, gender, race, and years of teaching. She also only answered the questions on the first page (1–5). She answered "yes" to questions 1, 2, 3, and 5. She further remarked that using varied teaching strategies enabled children to learn in a fun way, and that multicultural education is necessary to build self-esteem. The second teacher, who was also white, was fifty-nine years of age and had been in the system twenty-two years. She felt the goals of the program were adequately met and that using varied teaching strategies increased interest. In answer to question 3, she wrote that she already does role playing as a teaching method, but thought the dancing was great. Her response to multicultural education was that it is needed, but should be equitably distributed among cultures. She commented that AV resources were needed as well as outside programs and that the program was good but the timeframe for presentations was a bit lengthy. She thought there may be some frustration, but teachers would be receptive to learning if training was provided. With regard to racism and violence in the system she said that it was evident more in middle and high schools than elementary. She pointed out that "meaningful, ongoing curriculum interact positively at this school." She did not mention her multicultural education but said, "I have been teaching cross-culture respect throughout my career. Feelings are truly caught, not taught. Adults should set good examples." The third teacher, who is African American and forty-one years of age, was in her first year of teaching. She had graduated recently from an education certification, which required students to take a multicultural education course. Her answers were very detailed and as follows:

1. Yes/excellent, most children did not realize there were black people out West. The workshop helped to clarify this and the contents was something that can't be told to them enough.

2. Yes/excellent, it reaches all learning styles. The important thing is that they were having fun and didn't realize they were learning.

3. I try to use visual and audio, such as playing jazz as students work. I would strongly like teacher workshops demonstrating how to use the arts such as dance in the classroom.

4. It should be incorporated into every single aspect of the curriculum.

5. No, the school needs more textbooks with factual multicultural information.

6. Definitely, attitudes of some teachers toward students, information of text, and racism among the children.

7. Yes, because it is a long-awaited thing. Most important is that a lot of teachers are not comfortable teaching/lecturing in front of the classrooms. This way it is a more relaxed atmosphere, it's fun! (teachers like to have fun too).

8. For the most part they would be receptive.

9. Yes, superintendent and the school principal.

10. Not as of yet, but I will recap my classroom's diversity education for the year in the form of evaluation and discussion.

11. Four multicultural education related courses, not including an independent study.

The two social studies teachers who completed the survey from school #3 were both white females. One had been a teacher for nine years and the other a teacher for fifteen years. Both answered the questions similarly. Their overall outlook was that the program attained all of its goals and that using varied teaching strategies heightened interest. One teacher wrote that it was visual learning and allowed students to participate. Both said they would utilize the creative teaching strategies demonstrated, yet they felt there were not enough resources at the school. They each agreed that there is racism in the schools, and that the schools reflect society. Both suggested these types of workshops be offered throughout the system. One of the teachers said, "Of course! Only through education will we achieve a better understanding of each other and begin to value and accept each other's differences *and* similarities." As follow-up the teachers had discussions, one teacher also did art. Neither teacher had formal multicultural education.

Appendix C

National Efforts

THE NATIONAL CONFERENCE OF CHRISTIANS AND JEWS

According to its mission statement, "The National Conference of Christians and Jews, founded in 1927, is a human relations organization dedicated to fighting bias, bigotry and racism in America. The National Conference promotes understanding and respect among all races, regions and cultures through advocacy, conflict resolution and education."[1]

The National Conference works through sixty-three offices in thirty-two states and the District of Columbia in the areas of public education, communities, workplaces, and religious congregations. Its programming for public schools has been in diversity education. Some of these programs include The Multicultural Awareness Program (Tampa); The People Puzzle (interactive, multimedia exhibit for children aged three to eleven on diversity, prejudice, and discrimination/Northern Ohio Region and the Cleveland Children's Museum), and the distribution of the 1993 Brotherhood/Sisterhood resources (the "I Am America" poster and thirty-two-page educators' guide). The National Conference of Christians and Jews collaborates with and supports both national and local organizations, teacher associations, and student programming.

NATIONAL ASSOCIATION FOR MULTICULTURAL EDUCATION (NAME)

NAME was generated by the Association of Teacher Educators' Special Interest Group on Multicultural Education in 1990. It has now become a national organization that provides forums for debating cultural and racial issues for the purpose of expanding knowledge, stimulating research, and formulating educational policy in the field of multicultural education (Grant, 1992).

NAME sponsors an annual conference whose purpose is to "provide a forum for continuous and meaningful dialogue among participants as partners in multicultural education as they tackle the issue of diversity in American society and the world community, to exchange experience and professional expertise in each other's field; and to develop a network of dedicated educators that can function effectively to educate the community on multicultural concerns and diversity issues that we face in the 90's and the 21st century" (Grant, 1993–94, p. 4).

FACING HISTORY AND OURSELVES (FHAO)

FHAO was established in 1976. Its main office is based in Brookline, Massachusetts, with regional offices in Chicago, Illinois, and Memphis, Tennessee. The goal of FHAO is to target hatred, prejudice, racism, and indifference through the examination and teaching of the Jewish Holocaust and other case studies of mass extermination.

This organization has developed a curriculum entitled "The Holocaust and Human Behavior" for adolescents. The program reaches nearly half a million students each year in a variety of educational settings throughout the United States. Facing History provides educational workshops to teachers and other adult leaders. In turn, these trainees are able to offer the program in their local communities and schools.

Appendix D

Teacher Project: Preliminary Statistical Report

Anthony C. Stevens, Project Analyst

To prevent alpha inflation problems and [thereby] results that would be contaminated by capitalizing on chance, only the most pertinent questions were addressed in our analyses. We chose those questions that were capable of "telling the story" of the individuals' racist views and racist curriculum at once.

Relevant empirical results ranging from baseline figures to the results of a path analytic model that we believe will set a precedent for the study of antiracist curriculum and awareness are discussed below.

BASELINES BY GROUPS: PERCENT OF TEACHERS WHO AGREE WITH STATEMENT

Question 1: "Racism is defined as a system of privilege and penalty based on one's race."

Overall, 70.9 percent of the teachers surveyed agreed that racism is a system of privilege and penalty based on one's race. This is considered good news in that a proper definition of racism is necessary for individuals to understand and combat racism. Moreover, the sample used in this present study was not particularly diverse (70.6% were of European American descent) so there is a level of awareness previously unexpected by us. That of the two regions involved in this study (Midwest and New England) the Midwest teachers exhibited the most agreement with our definition of racism is indeed surprising. [The Midwest baseline for agreement with question one is 85.8% versus 59.9% for the New England teachers.] Intuitively, one might well have expected the reverse to be true.

The aforementioned baselines are encouraging. However, it must be noted that the overall baseline for disagreement with question 1 is 29.1 percent. In the present study this represents a small number of people (33) but the same percentage in a national sample of thousands presents an obvious problem. Clearly, an intensive educating process needs to be undertaken for the sake of all who suffer through racist views and corresponding curriculum.

The results were not void of absolute surprises. Consider the baselines regarding teacher birthplace and question 1. Of the four reported birthplace regions, the baselines for agreement with question 1 are as follows:

Midwest	88.0%
West	60.0%
South	100.0%
East	54.2%

Notice that *all* of the southern-born teachers agreed with question 1, as did nearly all of the Midwest-born teachers. These are the two regions in which many would expect to find the most opposition to diversity. It would seem that exposure to blatant racism *may* have contributed to a better understanding of what racism is for these teachers.

Question 3: "Racism is largely manifested in schools through biased curriculum and instruction."

Overall, only 49.5 percent of the teachers surveyed agreed that racism is largely manifested in schools through biased curriculum and instruction. This is where the heart of the matter lies and we clearly have work to do in this area.

Regionally, the baselines were quite similar for this question (51.6% and 48.0% agreement for New England and Midwest teachers respectively). By birthplace, it seems once again that the southern-born teachers know something the rest of them don't; 100 percent of the teachers from the South agreed with question 3 compared to baselines of 52.9 percent, 40 percent, and 46.2 percent from the Midwest, West, and East respectively.

Regarding ethnicity, only the teachers of color had an overwhelming amount of agreement with question 3 (baseline for agreement equals 81.2%). This suggests again that experiencing racism is the best way to be aware of it. All other U.S. teacher ethnic groups were below 50 percent agreement. Apparently, they think our curriculum choices are just fine, which of course is much of the problem.

Question 4: "Racism exists within most U.S. schools."

Strangely, the baseline for this question exhibits near perfection "across the board." Agreement for the total group was equal to 84.5 percent; 78.5 percent and 74.0 percent for the New England and Midwest teachers respectively; 80 percent and 90.6 percent for teachers of European descent and teachers of color respectively. Even the birthplace of the teachers didn't produce much baseline dispersion for this question (94.1% for Midwest-born, 100% for West- and southern-born, and 79.2% for East-born). The oddity is that so many teachers feel that racism exists in U.S. schools while so few believe that the *curriculum* itself is racist.

EMPIRICAL RESULTS

Reliability

The interitem correlation method (internal consistency) for scale reliability was conducted on the scale questions 1 through 34. The corresponding alpha coefficient was equal to 0.7820. This coefficient is considered very respectable for a preliminary questionnaire as many "well-established" questionnaires hold alpha coefficients equal to 0.80 and are deemed reliable.

Regressions

As expected, it was discovered that a teacher's score on certain variables could be used to predict scores on other variables. Those regressions that were significant are as follows:

Question 4 & Age

It was found that older teachers agreed more strongly with the statement that racism exists within most U.S. schools (question 4) than younger teachers did.   Consequently, it is possible to predict a teacher's answer to question 4 from his or her age.   Again it is proposed that having been exposed to blatant racism in one's life serves to heighten awareness.   Surely the older teachers have experienced blatant, nationwide racism in much stronger doses than the younger teachers have.

Question 25 & Question 27

It was found that teachers who grew up in families that promoted racist beliefs (question 27) reported having made unintentional racist/stereotypical comments (question 25) more than those who did not grow up in racist families.   This comes as no surprise, of course, but it reinforces the fact that we aren't born racists.   We learn racism.   Therefore, we can "unlearn" it.

T-tests

Group mean comparisons revealed statistically significant differences on several variables.   Those significant comparisons are as follows:

Males & Females

Question 5: "Racism in schools ended with the civil rights movement of the 1960s."   It was found that males agreed with this statement more than females did.

Elementary Teachers & Middle School Teachers

Question 4: "Racism exists in most U.S. schools."   It was found that middle school teachers agreed with this statement more than elementary school teachers did.

Question 5: "Racism in schools ended with the civil rights movement of the 1960s."   It was found that elementary school teachers agreed with this statement more than middle school teachers did.   An interesting case could be made here for the importance of psychological/social development.   It is certainly arguable that few if any individuals are more self-conscious than are middle school children.

Could it be that racist tendencies begin to manifest most strongly in this age group, at an age where "image is everything"?

Midwest Teachers & New England Teachers

Question 4: "Racism exists in most U.S. schools." It was found that Midwest schoolteachers agreed with this statement more than New England schoolteachers did.

Question 5: "Racism in schools ended with the civil rights movement of the 1960s." It was found that New England schoolteachers agreed with this statement more than the Midwest schoolteachers did. Of course, this helps explain the statistical differences found between the two groups on question 4.

The second part of the empirical report focuses on our pre test/post test mean comparisons. Statistically significant findings were found for the following:

- Question 3: "Racism is largely manifested in schools through biased curriculum and instruction."

- Question 6: "Being an antiracist teacher means paying attention to the *curriculum* in which some students may be favored over others."

- Question 25: "During your teaching career, you unintentionally made a racist/stereotypical comment to a student, parent, or fellow teacher."

In every case the participants' post test score moved significantly toward agreement with these questions, purportedly due to their exposure to the materials and training. The implication is that exposure to the antiracist curriculum materials increases awareness of racism, eliminating a "blindly racist" mind-set.

PATH ANALYSIS CONSTRUCTS

The unique capabilities of LISREL were called upon to estimate the paths of nine constructs that "fell out" of a factor analysis of the questionnaire (see Fig. 1). The predictor constructs are as follows:

1-Childhood Racist Experiences

2-Racism Awareness

3-Antiracist Education

4-Awareness of the Impact of Racism in Schools

The predicted constructs are as follows:

1-Racist Teaching Tendencies

2-Awareness of Antiracist Teaching Techniques

3-Openness to Antiracist Teaching Aids

4-Awareness of Antiracist Curriculum

5-Openness to Antiracist Curriculum

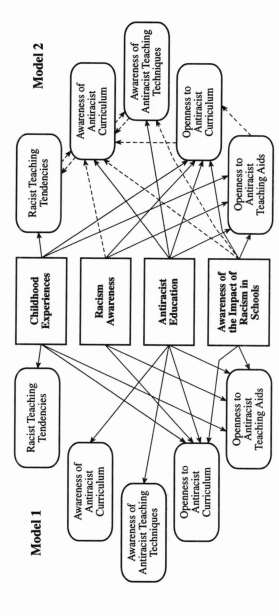

Figure 1. Models of path analysis results from the teacher race awareness study.

The unique capabilities of LISREL were called upon to estimate the paths of nine constructs that "fell out" of a factor analysis of the questionnaire. The predictor constructs are in bold in the center of the diagram, and the predicted constructs are in the rounded boxes along the outside.

Notes

INTRODUCTION

1. "New racism" is racial prejudice that can be practiced by any racial group or individual.

2. National Center for Education Statistics/Digest of Education Statistics (1992).

CHAPTER 1

1. Information obtained by the Equity Office/ Massachusetts Board of Education (1992).

CHAPTER 2

1. Visual and Performing Arts Curriculum Framework and Criteria Committee for California Public Schools: K–12, California State Department of Education, Sacramento, 1982.

2. These include, among many others, James A. Banks, Christine Bennett, Jim Cummins, Carl Grant, Sonia Nieto, and Christine Sleeter.

3. "In art history, courses rarely leave France, Italy, and sometimes England in considering the 'great' artists. What is called 'classical' music is classical only in Europe, not in Africa, Asia, or Latin America. This same ethnocentrism is found in our history books, which place Europeans and

European-Americans as the actors and all others as the recipients, bystanders, or bit players of history" (Nieto, 1996, p. 212).

4. This information is based on my twenty years of experience and communication with traditional artists.

CHAPTER 5

1. Audience evaluation survey, Branchard High School, June 1, 1993.

2. A disproportionate number of suspensions and detentions for students of color had been previously documented by a Branchard school committee member.

3. The audience evaluation survey asked each respondent to identify his or her race, gender, age, and status.

4. "Final Report Results from a Survey of Relationships," Branchard public schools, November 1992.

5. Suburban middle school performance, April 16, 1993.

APPENDIX C

1. *I Am American*; 1992 annual report, National Conference of Christians and Jews, Inc., 71 Fifth Avenue, NY, NY 10003.

References

Adams, Harold J. (1985). Multicultural nonsexist education. In Nicholas Colangelo, Dick Dustin, and Cecelia H. Foxley (Eds.), *Repression and recover: Fighting racism through education*, pp. 87–96.

Banks, James A. (1991). *Teaching strategies for ethnic studies*. (5th ed.). Boston: Allyn & Bacon.

Banks, James A. (1992, Fall). It's up to us. *Teaching Tolerance*, 20–23.

Bennett, Christine L. (1990). *Comprehensive multicultural education: Theory and practice*. (2nd ed.). Boston: Allyn & Bacon.

Bennett, Lerone, Jr. (1982). *Before the Mayflower*. Harmondsworth, Middlesex, England: Penguin Books.

Brown, Phyllis. (1995). Cultural identity groups overview and framework. Unpublished document, Fort River School, Amherst, MA.

Brown, Tony. (1995). *Black lies, white lies*. New York: William Morrow & Company.

Burns, Douglas. (1995, March 3). Student receives *Newsweek* honor. *The Daily Tribune*.

Carter, R. T., and Goodwin, L. (1994). Racial identity and education. *Review of Research in Education* 20, 291–336.

Chinn, Phillip C., and Gollnick, Donna M. (1994). *Multicultural education in a pluralistic society*. (4th ed.). Columbus, OH: Merrill Publishing Company.

Citron, Abraham F. (1977). *The "rightness" of "whiteness": The world of the white child in a segregated society*. Detroit, MI: Wayne State University, Publication of the Office of Urban Education, College of Education.

Clark, Christine E. (1993). *Multicultural education as a tool for disarming violence: A study through in-depth participatory action research*. Unpublished doctoral dissertation, University of Massachusetts, Amherst.

Cross, William E. (1991). *Shades of black: Diversity in African-American identity*. Philadelphia, PA: Temple University Press.

Curriculum for Restructuring Education and New Teaching Strategies (CURRENTS). (1992). *Collaboratives for humanities and arts teaching (chart)*. PA: PROPEL.

Cushner, Kenneth, McClelland, Averil, and Safford, Phillip. (1992). *Human diversity in education: An integrative approach*. New York: McGraw-Hill.

Daniel, Yvonne P. (1984). *What is ethnic dance?* Ethnic dance festival program, San Francisco City Celebration, pp. 14–15.

Daniel, Yvonne P. (1990, March). *A pluralist's view of multicultural education or towards the creation of new structures through dance/musics*. Unpublished manuscript, Smith College, Dance Department, Northampton, MA.

Delpit, Lisa D. (1988). *The silenced dialogue: Power and pedagogy in educating other people's children*. In N. Hidalgo, C. L. McDowell, and E. V. Siddle (Eds.), *Facing racism in education*. Cambridge, MA: *Harvard Educational Review*; reprint series no. 21.

Donaldson, Karen B. (1992). *Multicultural arts survey/Branchard (pseudonym) Elementary School pilot survey*. Unpublished manuscript.

Donaldson, Karen B. (1993a). *Racism and violence in U.S. schools: Lessons from two school systems*. Unpublished manuscript.

Donaldson, Karen B. (1993b). *The role of the arts in multicultural education*. Unpublished manuscript.

Donaldson, Karen B. (1994, Winter). Through students' eyes. *Multicultural Education*, 26–28.

Donaldson, K. (1995, May). "Charissa" Midwest Student Interview.

Donaldson, K. (1995, August). "Charissa" Midwest Student Interview.

Donaldson, K. (1995, Spring). "Nichelle" Midwest Student Interview.

Donaldson, K. (1995, Fall). "Katina" Midwest Student Interview.

Donaldson, Karen B., and Visani, Maurizio. (1995). Middle school multicultural club report. Unpublished document.

Educators' Handbook. (1987). *A research perspective*. Virginia Richardson-Koehler (Senior Ed.). New York: Longman Publishers.

Feagin, Joe R., and Vera, Hernan. (1995). *White racism*. New York: Routledge Publishers.

Fine, Michelle. (1991). *Framing drop-outs: Notes on the politics of an urban public high school*. Albany: State University of New York Press.

Fordham, Signithia, and Ogbu, John U. (1986). Black students' school success: Coping with the burden of acting white. *The Urban Review* 18(3).

Foster, Michele. (1993). Resisting racism: Personal testimonies of African American teachers. In Michelle Fine and Lois Weis (Eds.), *Beyond silenced voices: Class, race, and gender in United States schools*, pp. 273–88. Albany: State University of New York Press.

Fry, Finnegan. (1990). *Living our commitments: A handbook for whites joining together to identify, own and dismantle our racist conditioning*. Unpublished handbook.

Garcia, Ricardo L. (1991). *Teaching in a pluralistic society: Concepts, models, strategies*. (2nd ed.). New York: HarperCollins Publishers.

Gardner, Howard. (1983). *Frames of mind: The theory of multiple intelligences*. New York: Basic Books.

Gardner, Howard. (1993). *Multiple intelligences: The theory in practice*. New York: Basic Books.

Gay, Geneva. (1990, September). Achieving educational equality through curriculum desegregation. *Phi Delta Kappan*, 56–62.

Gibson, Margaret A. (1976, November). Approaches to multicultural education in the United States: Some concepts and assumptions. *Anthropology and Education Quarterly* 4(15).

Grant, Carl A. (Ed.). (1992). *Research and multicultural education*. London: Falmer Press.

Grant, Carl A. (1993–94). From the president. *The Magazine of the National Association for Multicultural Education*: Premiere issue. Fort Atkinson, WI: Highsmith Press.

Grant, Carl A., and Sleeter, Christine E. (1987, November). An analysis of multicultural education in the United States. *Harvard Educational Review* 57(4), 421–43.

Gross, Jane, and Smothers, Ronald. (1994, August 15). In prom dispute, a town's race divisions emerge. *The New York Times*.

Hamilton, H., and Worswick, C. (Eds.) (1982a). *Patterns of racism*. Institute of Race Relations. New York.

Hamilton, H., and Worswick, C. (Eds.). (1982b). *Roots of racism*. Institute of Race Relations. New York.

Hart, Thomas E., and Lumsden, Linda. (1989, May). *Confronting racism in the schools*. Oregon School Study Council, University of Oregon, ED 306 705.

Helms, J. E. (Ed). (1990). *Black and white racial identity: Theory, research and practice*. Westport, CT: Greenwood Press.

Hesler, Marjorie W. (1987, December). Communication strategies for the multicultural class. *U.S. Department of Education*, Microfilm ED 293 176 12.

Hidalgo, Nitza M., McDowell, Ceasar L., and Siddle, Emilie V. (Eds.). (1992). *Facing racism in education*. Cambridge, MA: *Harvard Educational Review*.

Inhabiting Other Lives. (1992). (Dade County Florida). *Collaboratives for humanities and arts teaching*. PA: PROPEL.

Jenoure, Theresa. (1993, April). *Implications of social and political art for school reform*. Unpublished manuscript, School of Education, CDCR Program, University of Massachusetts, Amherst.

Kailin, Julie. (1994). Anti-racist staff development for teachers: Considerations of race, class, and gender. *Teacher & Teaching Education* 10(2), 169–84.

Keil, Charles. (1985). *Paideia con salsa*: Ancient Greek education for active citizenship and the role of Latin dance-music in our schools. In David McAllester (Ed.), *Becoming human through music*, chap. 9. Reston, VA: Music Educators National Conference.

Kendall, Frances E. (1996). *Diversity in the classroom: A multicultural approach to education of young children*. (2nd ed.). New York & London: Teachers College Press.

King, J. E. (1991). Dysconscious racism: Ideology, identity, and the miseducation of teachers. *Journal of Negro Education* 60(2), 133–46.

Kozol, Jonathan. (1991). *Savage inequalities: Children in America's schools*. New York: Harper Perennial.

Kromkowski, John A. (Ed.). (1993). *Annual editions: Race and ethnic relations 93/94*. Guilford, CT: Dushkin Publishing.

Ladson-Billings, G. (1994). *The dreamkeepers: Successful teachers of African American children*. San Francisco: Jossey-Bass Publishers.

Lawrence, Sandra, and Tatum, Beverly. (1995). White educators as allies: Moving from awareness to action. In Michelle Fine and Linda Powell (Eds.), *Offwhite: Critical perspectives on race*. New York: Routledge Publishers.

LeCompte, Margaret Diane, and Dworkin, Anthony Gary. (1991). *Giving up on school: Student dropouts and teacher burnouts*. Newbury Park, CA: Corwin Press.

Lovano-Kerr, Jessie, and Zimmerman, Enid. (1977, January). Multiculture teacher education program in the arts. *Art Education*, 34–38.

McCarthy, Cameron. (1988, August). Rethinking liberal and radical perspectives on racial inequality in schooling: Making the case of nonsynchrony. *Harvard Educational Review* 58(3), 265–79.

McCormick, Theresa M. (1984, Fall). A two-point perspective on art: Multicultural-nonsexist education. *Educational Considerations* 11(2), 17–19.

McCormick, Theresa M. (1986, Fall). Multicultural education and competency testing—conflicts and consequences. *Urban Educator* 8(1), 31–42.

McCormick, Theresa M. (1994). *Creating the nonsexist classroom: A multicultural approach*. New York: Teachers College Press.

McIntosh, Peggy. (1988). *White privilege and male privilege: A personal account of coming to see correspondences through work in womens studies*. Working paper no. 189, Wellesley College, Center for Research on Women, Wellesley, MA.

Medina, Noe, and D. Monty, Neill. (1990). *Fallout from the testing explosion*. (3rd ed.). Cambridge, MA: Fair Test.

Mizell, Linda. (1992). *Think about racism*. New York: Walker & Company.

Molnar, Alex. (1989, October). Racism in America: A continuing dilemma. *Educational Leadership*, 71–72.

Multicultural Education. (1993, Summer). *The Magazine of the National Association for Multicultural Education:* Premiere issue. Fort Atkinson, WI: Highsmith Press.

Murray, Carolyn B., and Clark, Reginald M. (1990, June). Targets of racism. *The American School Board Journal*.

National Center for Education Statistics. (1990–91). Schools and staffing survey (SASS). U.S. Department of Education.

National Center for Education Statistics/Digest of Education Statistics. (1992). *University of Massachusetts Reference Book*.

National Conference of Christians and Jews. (1992). *I am America*. New York.

Nieto, Sonia. (1994a, Winter). Lessons from students on creating a chance to dream. *Harvard Education Review* 64(4), 392–426.

Nieto, Sonia. (1994b, Spring). Affirmation, solidarity, and critique: Moving beyond tolerance in multicultural education. *Multicultural Education*, 9–12, 35–38.

Nieto, Sonia. (1996). *Affirming diversity: The sociopolitical context of multicultural education*. (2nd ed.). New York: Longman Publishers.

Oakes, Jeannie. (1986, September). Keeping track, part 1: The policy and practice of curriculum inequality. *Phi Delta Kappan*, 12–17.

Pharr, Suzanne. (1988). *The common elements of oppressions in homophobia: A weapon of sexism*. Little Rock, AR: The Women's Project.

Pine, Gerald J., and Hilliard, Asa G. (1990, April). Rx for racism: Imperatives for America's schools. *Phi Delta Kappan*, 593–600.

Ramsey, Patricia G. (1987). *Teaching and learning in a diverse world: Multicultural education for young children*. New York & London: Teachers College Press.

Readings on Equal Education. (1986). Volume 9: Education policy in an era of conservative reform (introduction). AMS Press, Inc., Microfilm ED 299 686.

Reiman, Jeffrey. (1990). *The rich get richer and the poor get prison: Ideology, class, and criminal justice*. New York: Macmillan Publishing.

Rist, Ray C. (1971). *Student social class and teacher expectations: The self-fulfilling prophecy in ghetto education.* Cambridge, MA: *Harvard Educational Review*; reprint series, no. 5.

Rosenburg, Howard. (1979, February). The art of the popular film adds depth to multicultural studies. *Art Education*, 10–14.

Rubin, Janet E., and Ruffin, Roosevelt. (1993). Drama/theatre and multicultural education. *Proteus: A Journal of Ideas*, 10(1).

Ruenzel, David (1994, August). Blackflight. *Teacher Magazine*, 19–23.

Seidman, I. E. (1991). *Interviewing as qualitative research.* New York: Teachers College Press.

Sleeter, Christine E. (1991). *Empowerment through multicultural education.* Albany: State University of New York Press.

Sleeter, Christine E. (1992). *Keepers of the American dream: A study of staff development and multicultural education.* London: Falmer Press.

Sleeter, Christine E. (1994, Spring). White racism. *Multicultural Education* 1(4), 5–8, 39.

Stover, Del. (1990, June). The new racism. *The American School Board Journal*, 14–18.

Study School Department. (1992). *A final report on results from a survey of relationships (student race relations).*

Tatum, Beverly Daniel. (1987). *Assimilation blues: Black families in a white community.* Northampton, MA: Hazel-Maxwell Publishing.

Tatum, Beverly Daniel. (1992, Winter). Teaching the psychology of racism. *Mount Holyoke Alumnae Quarterly*, 19–21.

Tatum, Beverly Daniel. (1993). *Teaching white students about racism: The search for white allies and the restoration of hope.* Manuscript submitted for publication, Department of Psychology and Education, Mount Holyoke College, South Hadley, MA.

Taylor, Anne. (1973). A report of a miniconference—Taos, New Mexico. *Art Education*, 9–13.

United States Society for Education through Art (USSEA). (1992, June). *Newsletter* 16(2).

Visual and Performing Arts Curriculum Framework and Criteria Committee. (1982). *Visual and performing arts framework for California public schools: Kindergarten through grade twelve.* California State Board of Education.

Wasson, Robyn F., Stuhr, Patricia L., and Petrovich-Mwaniki, Lois. (1990). Teaching art in the multicultural classroom: Six position statements. *Studies in Art Education: A Journal of Issues and Research* 31(4), 234–46.

Wasson, Robyn F., Stuhr, Patricia L., and Petrovich-Mwaniki, Lois. (1992, January). Curriculum guidelines for the multicultural art classroom. *Art Education*, 16–24.

Weinberg, Meyer. (1990). *Racism in the United States: A comprehensive classified bibliography*. Westport, CT: Greenwood Press.

Wheelock, Anne. (1992). *Crossing the tracks: How untracking can save America's schools*. New York: New York Press.

Wilson, Amos N. (1987). *The developmental psychology of the black child*. New York: Africana Research Publications.

Wyman, Ray. (1991). *Media systems*. Course notes, School of Education, University of Massachusetts, Amherst.

Index

About the Author

KAREN B. McLEAN DONALDSON is Assistant Professor in the Curriculum and Instruction Department/College of Education at Iowa State University. She has worked as a multicultural education specialist for 15 years and is president of Multicultural Education Development, Inc.

ISBN 0-275-95478-1

90000>

9 780275 954789

HARDCOVER BAR CODE